WITHDRAWN AUG 0 1 2011

STAR WARS®

THE CLONE WARS™

HERO OF THE CONFEDERACY

DESIGNER **STEPHEN REICHERT**

ASSISTANT EDITOR **FREDDYE LINS**

EDITOR **RANDY STRADLEY**

PUBLISHER **MIKE RICHARDSON**

Special thanks to Jann Moorhead, David Anderman, Troy Alders, Leland Chee, Sue Rostoni, and Carol Roeder at Lucas Licensing.

Published by Dark Horse Books, a division of Dark Horse Comics, Inc.
10956 SE Main Street, Milwaukie, OR 97222

darkhorse.com | starwars.com

To find a comics shop in your area, call the Comic Shop Locator Service toll-free at 1.888.266.4226
First edition: September 2010 | ISBN 978-1-59582-552-0

Library of Congress Cataloging-in-Publication Data

Gilroy, Henry.
Star wars, the clone wars : hero of the confederacy / script, Henry Gilroy, Steven Melching ; pencils, Brian Koschak ; inks, Dan Parsons.
     p. cm.
"This volume collects issues #10–#12 of the Dark Horse comic-book series Star Wars: The Clone Wars."
ISBN 978-1-59582-552-0
1. Star Wars fiction--Comic books, strips, etc. 2. Graphic novels. I. Melching, Steven. II. Koschak, Brian. III. Star Wars, the clone wars (Television program) IV. Title. V. Title: Clone Wars.
PN6728.S73G55 2010
741.5'973--dc22

                            2010013061

10 9 8 7 6 5 4 3 2 1

NOV 2 1 2011

Printed at 1010 Printing International, Ltd., Guangdong Province, China

president **Mike Richardson** • executive vice president **Neil Hankerson** • chief financial officer **Tom Weddle** • vice president of publishing **Randy Stradley** • vice president of business development **Michael Martens** • vice president of marketing, sales, and licensing **Anita Nelson** • vice president of product development **David Scroggy** • vice president of information technology **Dale LaFountain** • director of purchasing **Darlene Vogel** • general counsel **Ken Lizzi** • editorial director **Davey Estrada** • senior managing editor **Scott Allie** • senior books editor **Chris Warner** • executive editor **Diana Schutz** • director of design and production **Cary Grazzini** • art director **Lia Ribacchi** • director of scheduling **Cara Niece**

STAR WARS: THE CLONE WARS—HERO OF THE CONFEDERACY

This volume collects issues #10–#12 of the Dark Horse comic-book series *Star Wars: The Clone Wars*.

THE CLONE WARS

HERO OF THE CONFEDERACY

SCRIPT **HENRY GILROY**
STEVEN MELCHING

PENCILS **BRIAN KOSCHAK**

INKS **DAN PARSONS**

COLORS **MICHAEL E. WIGGAM**

LETTERING **MICHAEL HEISLER**

COVER ART **SCOTT HEPBURN**
with **MICHAEL E. WIGGAM**

DARK HORSE BOOKS®

THE RISE OF THE EMPIRE
1000–0 YEARS BEFORE *STAR WARS: A NEW HOPE*

The events in these stories take place approximately
twenty-two years before the Battle of Yavin.

After the seeming final defeat of the Sith, the Republic enters a state
of complacency. In the waning years of the Republic, the Senate is rife
with corruption, and the ambitious Senator Palpatine has himself elected
Supreme Chancellor. This is the era of the prequel trilogy.

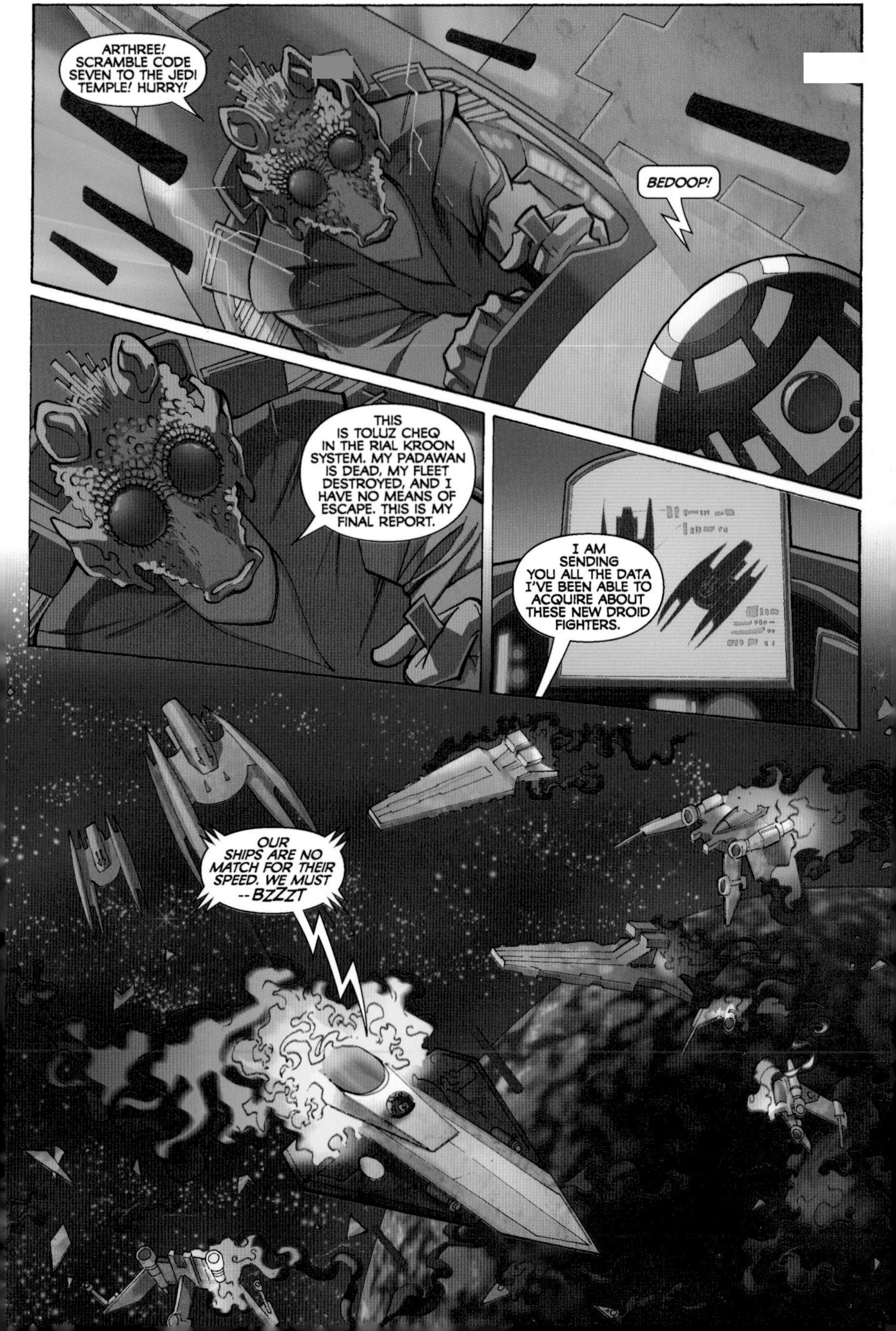
ARTHREE! SCRAMBLE CODE SEVEN TO THE JEDI TEMPLE! HURRY!
BEDOOP!
THIS IS TOLUZ CHEQ IN THE RIAL KROON SYSTEM. MY PADAWAN IS DEAD, MY FLEET DESTROYED, AND I HAVE NO MEANS OF ESCAPE. THIS IS MY FINAL REPORT.
I AM SENDING YOU ALL THE DATA I'VE BEEN ABLE TO ACQUIRE ABOUT THESE NEW DROID FIGHTERS.
OUR SHIPS ARE NO MATCH FOR THEIR SPEED. WE MUST --BZZZT

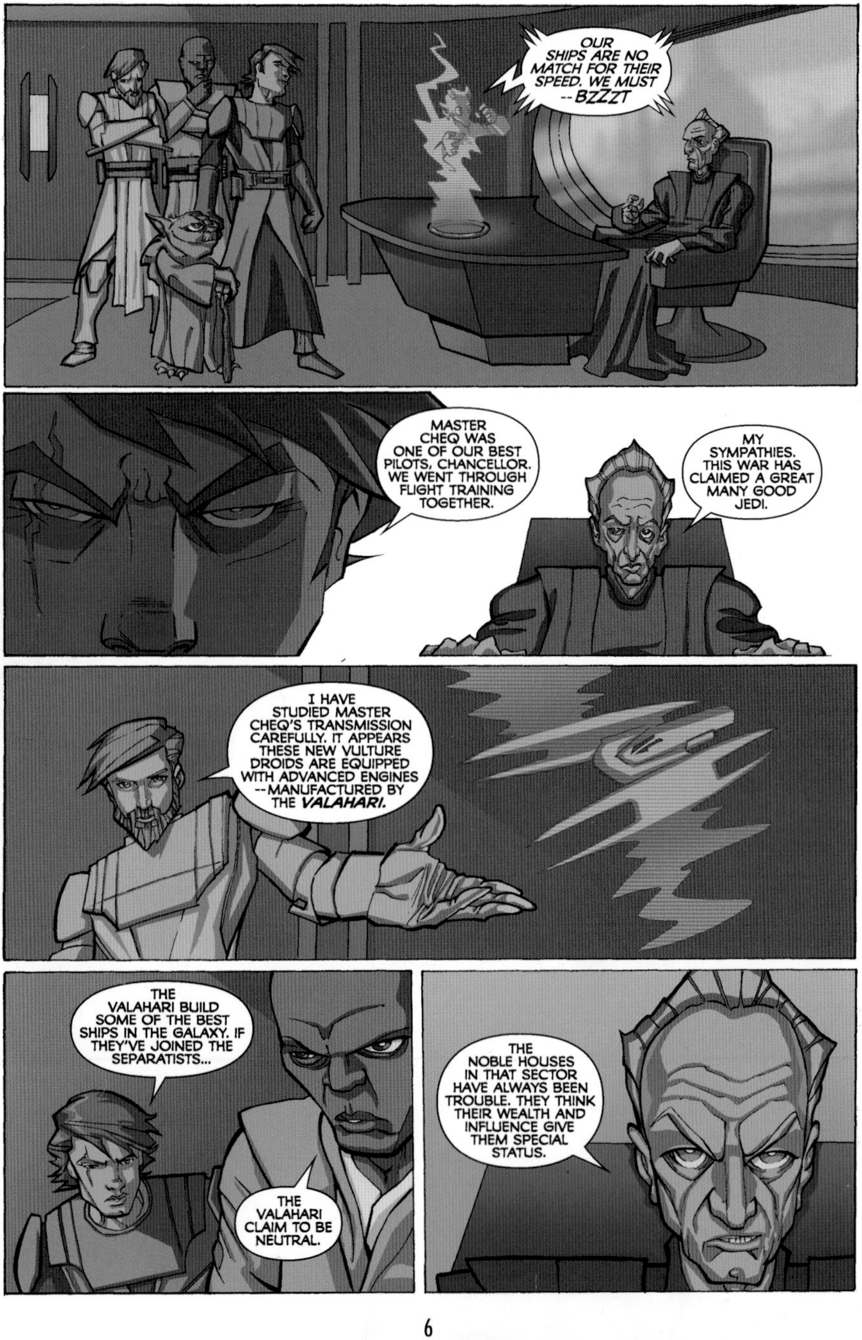
OUR SHIPS ARE NO MATCH FOR THEIR SPEED. WE MUST --BZZZT
MASTER CHEQ WAS ONE OF OUR BEST PILOTS, CHANCELLOR. WE WENT THROUGH FLIGHT TRAINING TOGETHER.
MY SYMPATHIES. THIS WAR HAS CLAIMED A GREAT MANY GOOD JEDI.
I HAVE STUDIED MASTER CHEQ'S TRANSMISSION CAREFULLY. IT APPEARS THESE NEW VULTURE DROIDS ARE EQUIPPED WITH ADVANCED ENGINES --MANUFACTURED BY THE VALAHARI.
THE VALAHARI BUILD SOME OF THE BEST SHIPS IN THE GALAXY. IF THEY'VE JOINED THE SEPARATISTS...
THE VALAHARI CLAIM TO BE NEUTRAL.
THE NOBLE HOUSES IN THAT SECTOR HAVE ALWAYS BEEN TROUBLE. THEY THINK THEIR WEALTH AND INFLUENCE GIVE THEM SPECIAL STATUS.

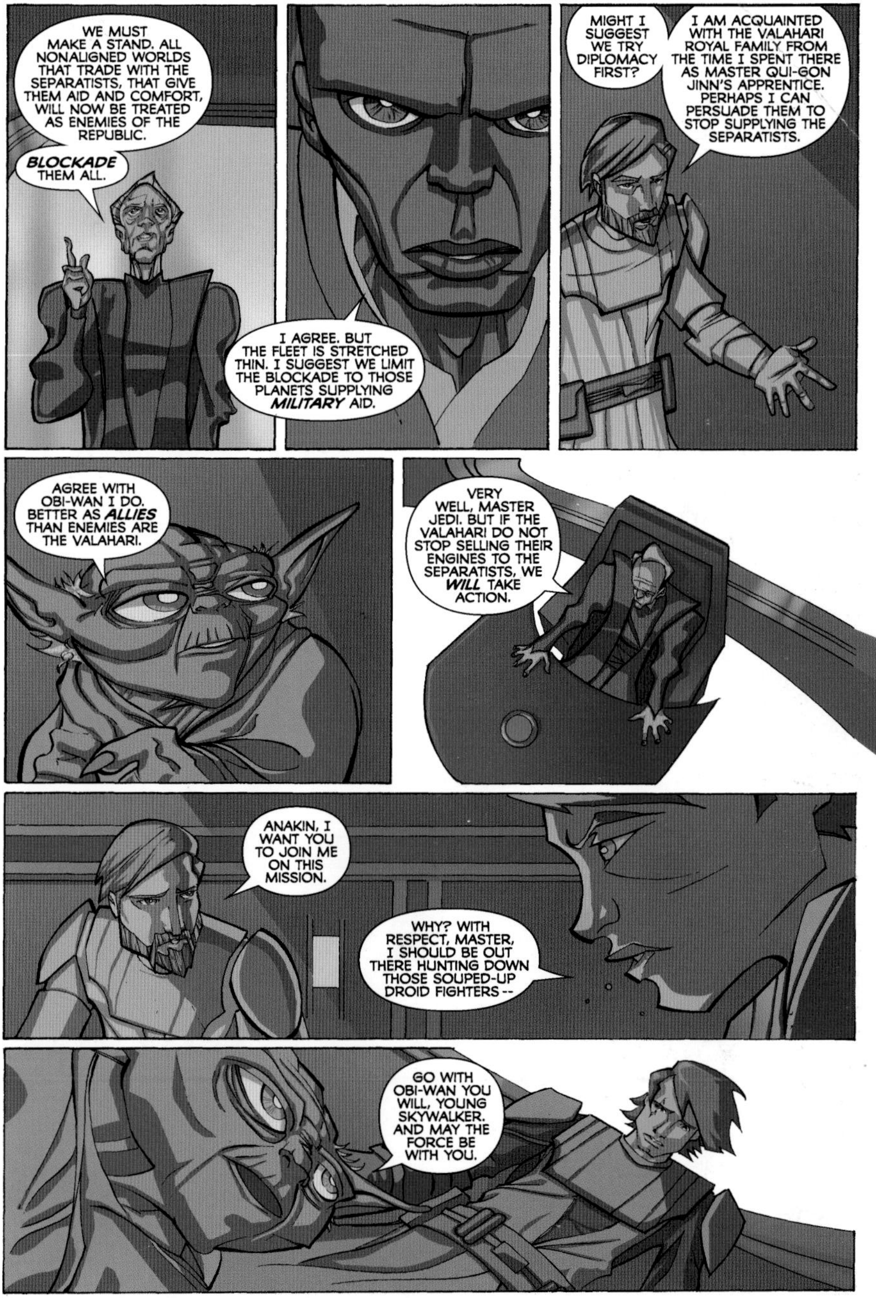
WE MUST MAKE A STAND. ALL NONALIGNED WORLDS THAT TRADE WITH THE SEPARATISTS, THAT GIVE THEM AID AND COMFORT, WILL NOW BE TREATED AS ENEMIES OF THE REPUBLIC.
BLOCKADE THEM ALL.
I AGREE. BUT THE FLEET IS STRETCHED THIN. I SUGGEST WE LIMIT THE BLOCKADE TO THOSE PLANETS SUPPLYING *MILITARY* AID.
MIGHT I SUGGEST WE TRY DIPLOMACY FIRST?
I AM ACQUAINTED WITH THE VALAHARI ROYAL FAMILY FROM THE TIME I SPENT THERE AS MASTER QUI-GON JINN'S APPRENTICE. PERHAPS I CAN PERSUADE THEM TO STOP SUPPLYING THE SEPARATISTS.
AGREE WITH OBI-WAN I DO. BETTER AS *ALLIES* THAN ENEMIES ARE THE VALAHARI.
VERY WELL, MASTER JEDI. BUT IF THE VALAHARI DO NOT STOP SELLING THEIR ENGINES TO THE SEPARATISTS, WE *WILL* TAKE ACTION.
ANAKIN, I WANT YOU TO JOIN ME ON THIS MISSION.
WHY? WITH RESPECT, MASTER, I SHOULD BE OUT THERE HUNTING DOWN THOSE SOUPED-UP DROID FIGHTERS --
GO WITH OBI-WAN YOU WILL, YOUNG SKYWALKER. AND MAY THE FORCE BE WITH YOU.

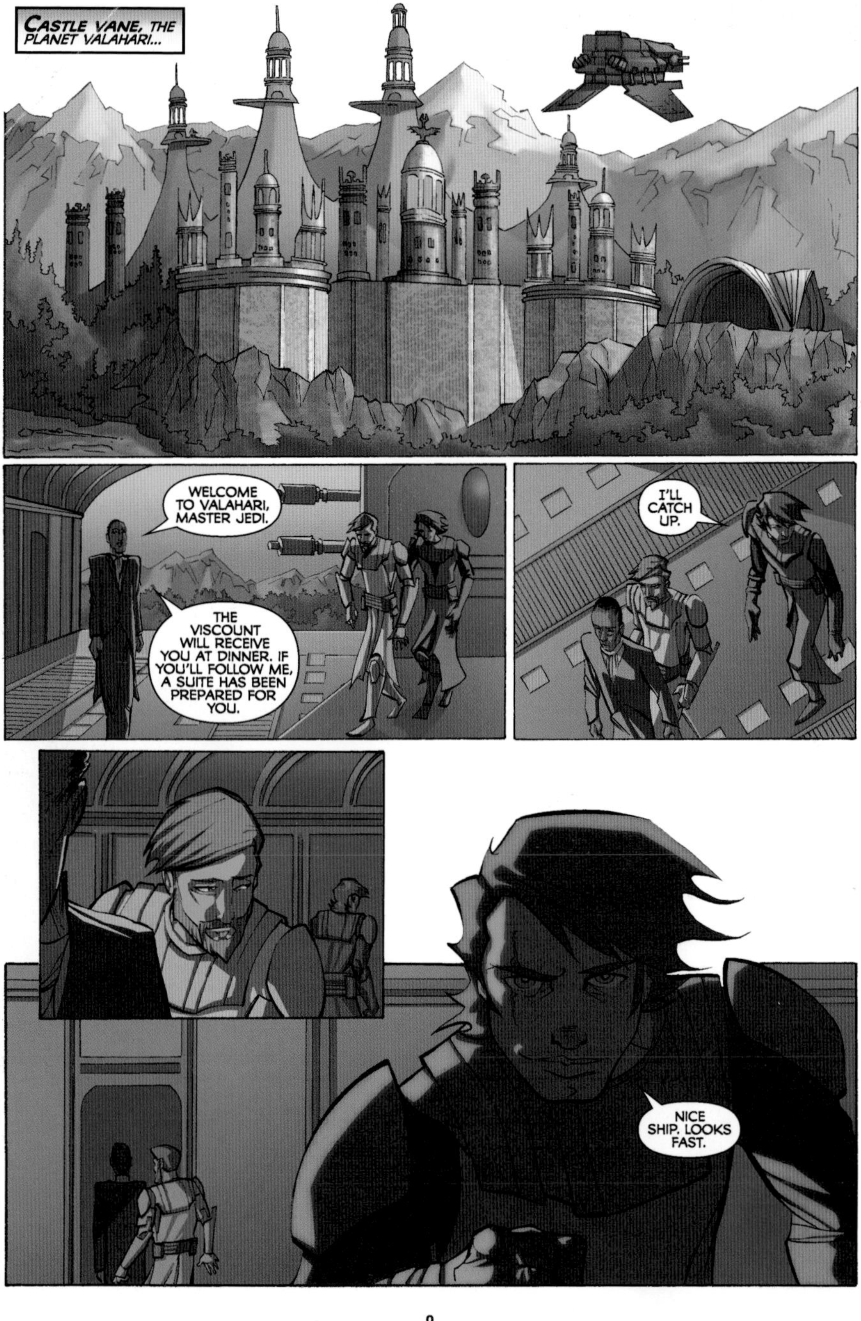
CASTLE VANE, THE PLANET VALAHARI...
WELCOME TO VALAHARI, MASTER JEDI.
THE VISCOUNT WILL RECEIVE YOU AT DINNER. IF YOU'LL FOLLOW ME, A SUITE HAS BEEN PREPARED FOR YOU.
I'LL CATCH UP.
NICE SHIP. LOOKS FAST.

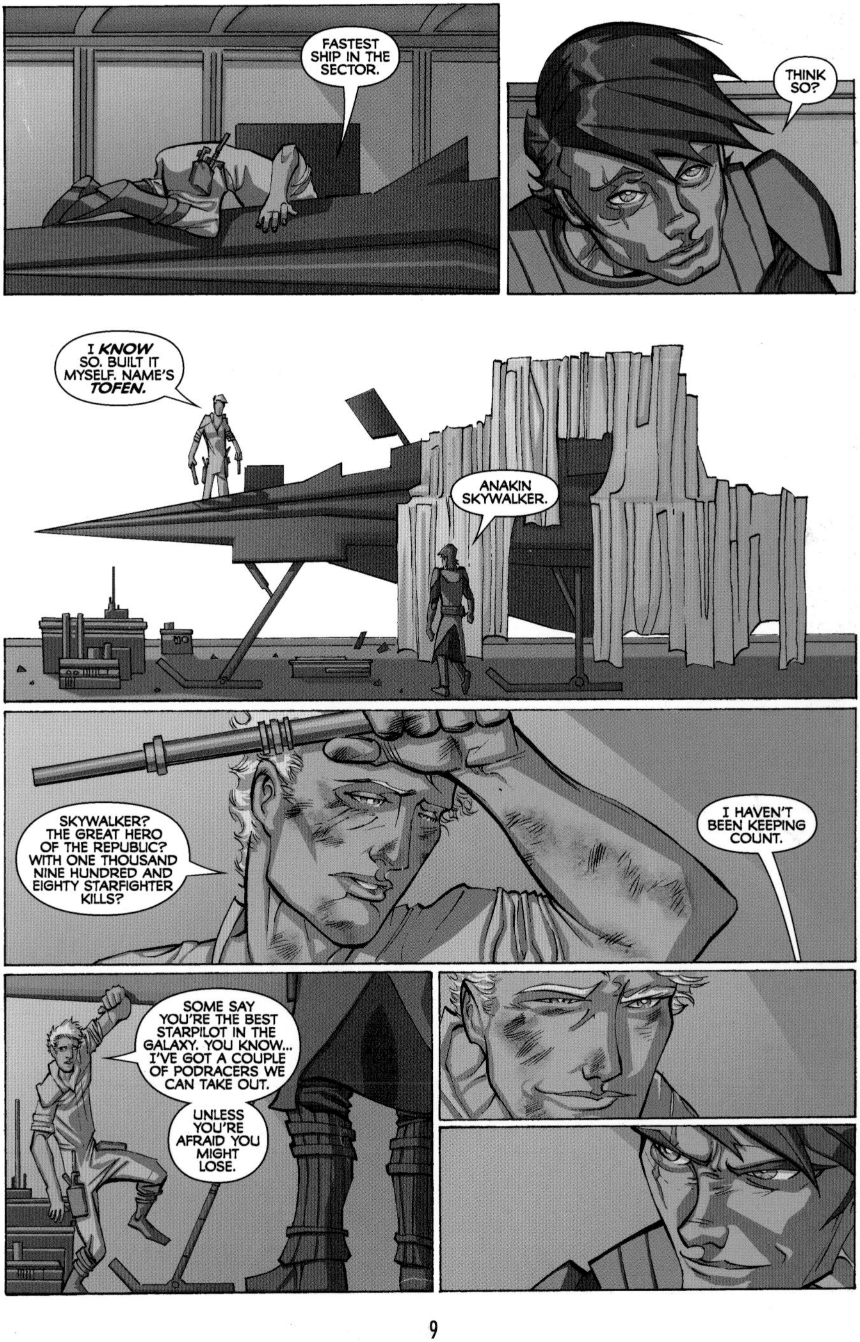
FASTEST SHIP IN THE SECTOR.
THINK SO?
I KNOW SO. BUILT IT MYSELF. NAME'S TOFEN.
ANAKIN SKYWALKER.
SKYWALKER? THE GREAT HERO OF THE REPUBLIC? WITH ONE THOUSAND NINE HUNDRED AND EIGHTY STARFIGHTER KILLS?
I HAVEN'T BEEN KEEPING COUNT.
SOME SAY YOU'RE THE BEST STARPILOT IN THE GALAXY. YOU KNOW... I'VE GOT A COUPLE OF PODRACERS WE CAN TAKE OUT.
UNLESS YOU'RE AFRAID YOU MIGHT LOSE.

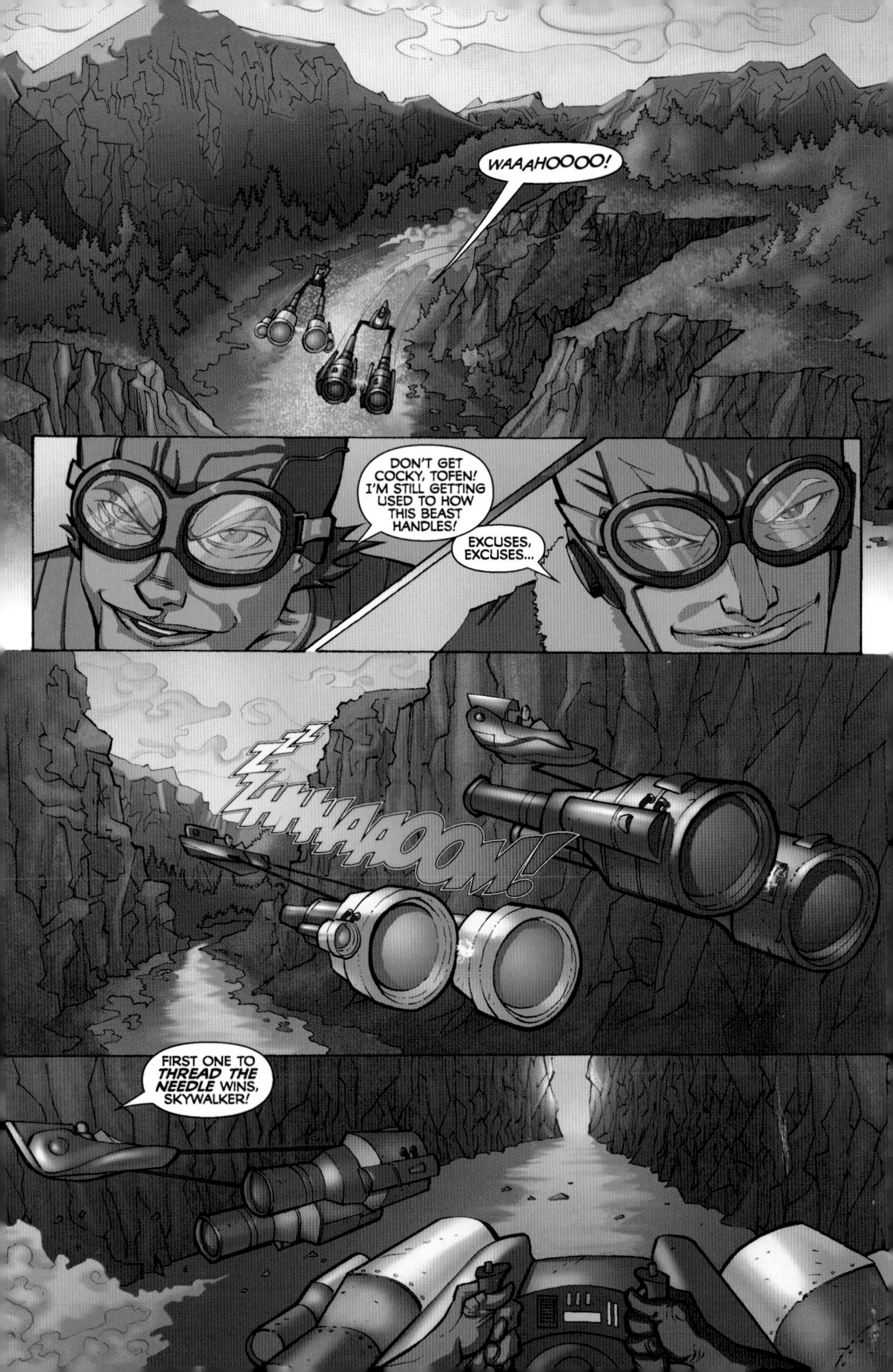
WAAAHOOOO!
DON'T GET COCKY, TOFEN! I'M STILL GETTING USED TO HOW THIS BEAST HANDLES!
EXCUSES, EXCUSES...
ZZZHHAROOM!
FIRST ONE TO THREAD THE NEEDLE WINS, SKYWALKER!

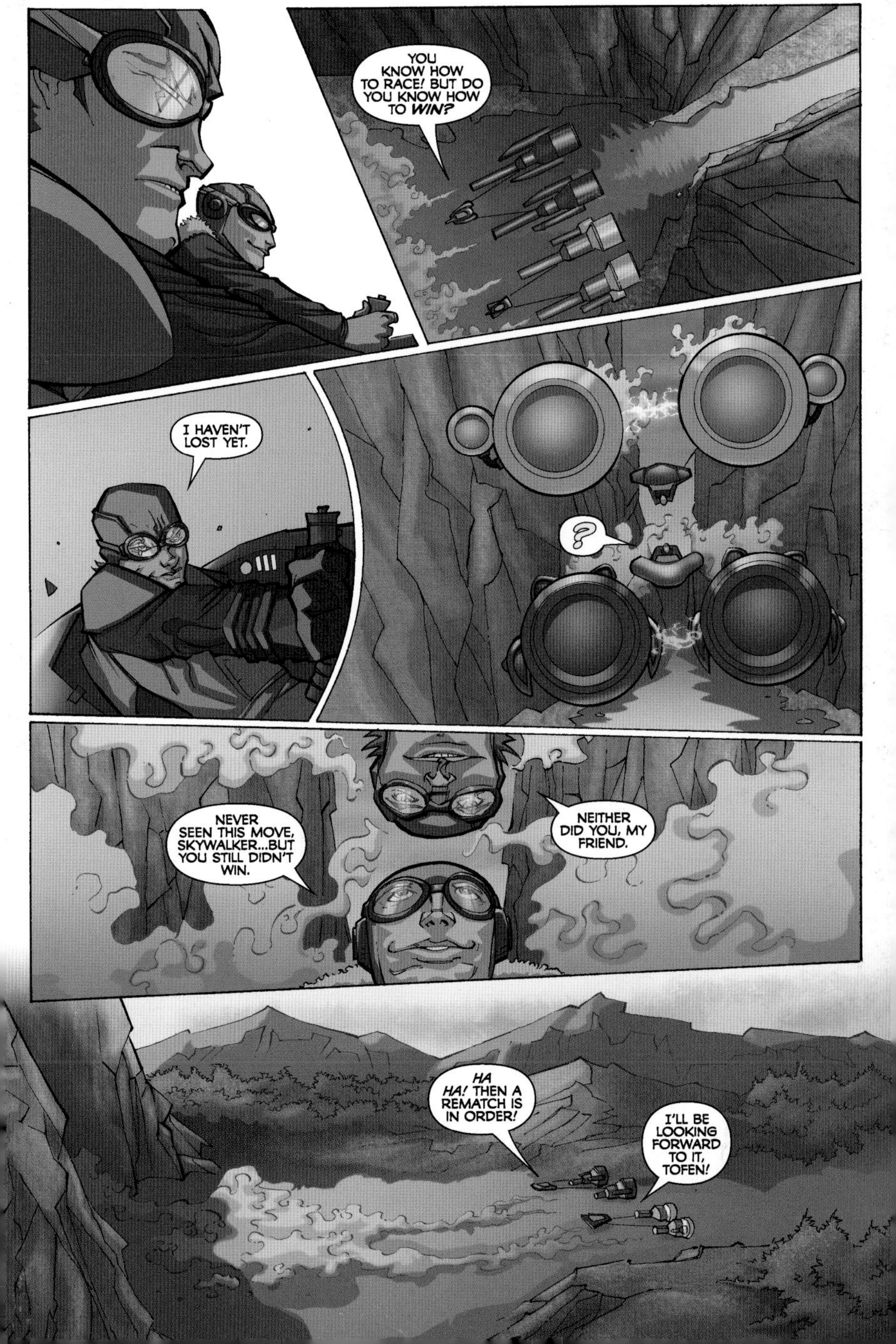
YOU KNOW HOW TO RACE! BUT DO YOU KNOW HOW TO WIN?
I HAVEN'T LOST YET.
?
NEVER SEEN THIS MOVE, SKYWALKER...BUT YOU STILL DIDN'T WIN.
NEITHER DID YOU, MY FRIEND.
HA HA! THEN A REMATCH IS IN ORDER!
I'LL BE LOOKING FORWARD TO IT, TOFEN!

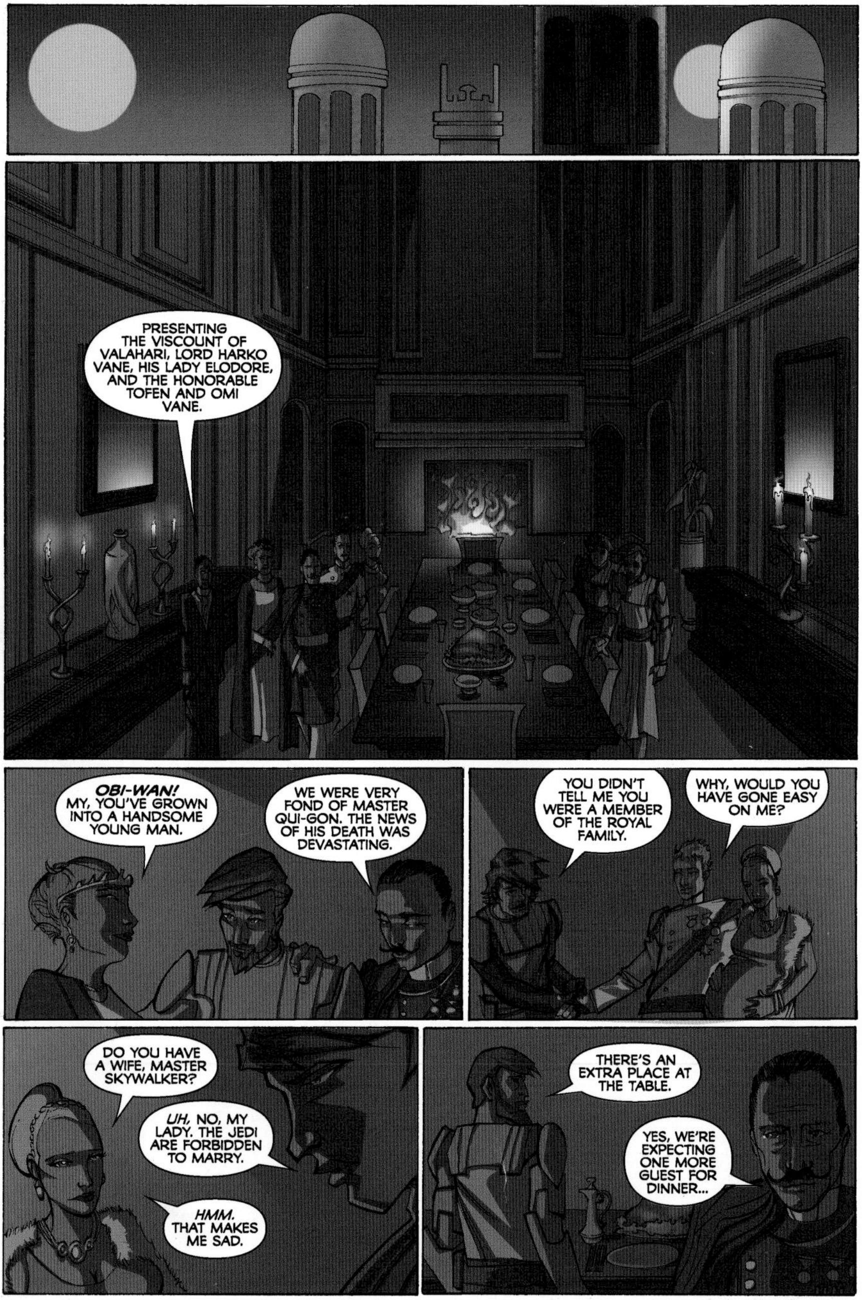
PRESENTING THE VISCOUNT OF VALAHARI, LORD HARKO VANE, HIS LADY ELODORE, AND THE HONORABLE TOFEN AND OMI VANE.
OBI-WAN! MY, YOU'VE GROWN INTO A HANDSOME YOUNG MAN.
WE WERE VERY FOND OF MASTER QUI-GON. THE NEWS OF HIS DEATH WAS DEVASTATING.
YOU DIDN'T TELL ME YOU WERE A MEMBER OF THE ROYAL FAMILY.
WHY, WOULD YOU HAVE GONE EASY ON ME?
DO YOU HAVE A WIFE, MASTER SKYWALKER?
UH, NO, MY LADY. THE JEDI ARE FORBIDDEN TO MARRY.
HMM. THAT MAKES ME SAD.
THERE'S AN EXTRA PLACE AT THE TABLE.
YES, WE'RE EXPECTING ONE MORE GUEST FOR DINNER...

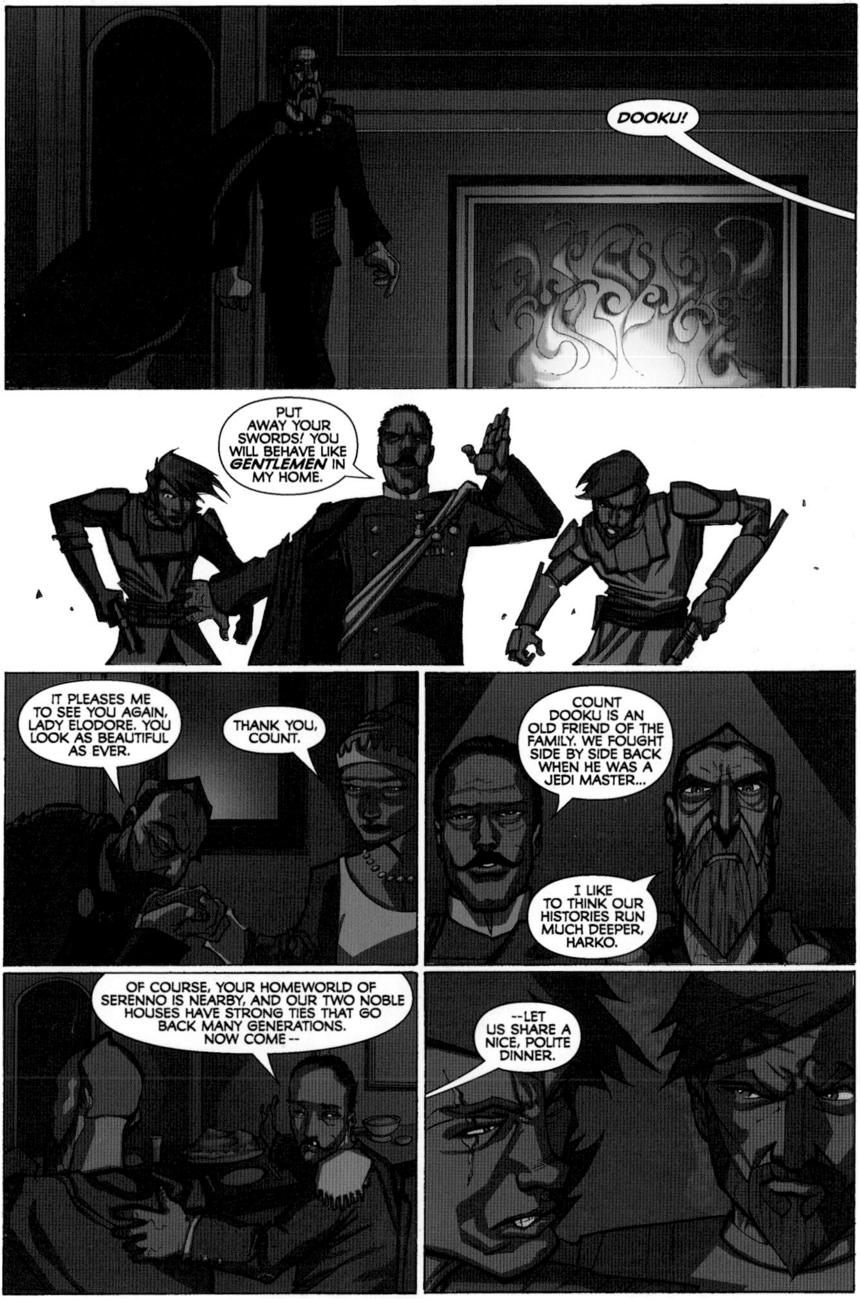
DOOKU!
PUT AWAY YOUR SWORDS! YOU WILL BEHAVE LIKE *GENTLEMEN* IN MY HOME.
IT PLEASES ME TO SEE YOU AGAIN, LADY ELODORE. YOU LOOK AS BEAUTIFUL AS EVER.
THANK YOU, COUNT.
COUNT DOOKU IS AN OLD FRIEND OF THE FAMILY. WE FOUGHT SIDE BY SIDE BACK WHEN HE WAS A JEDI MASTER...
I LIKE TO THINK OUR HISTORIES RUN MUCH DEEPER, HARKO.
OF COURSE, YOUR HOMEWORLD OF SERENNO IS NEARBY, AND OUR TWO NOBLE HOUSES HAVE STRONG TIES THAT GO BACK MANY GENERATIONS. NOW COME --
--LET US SHARE A NICE, POLITE DINNER.

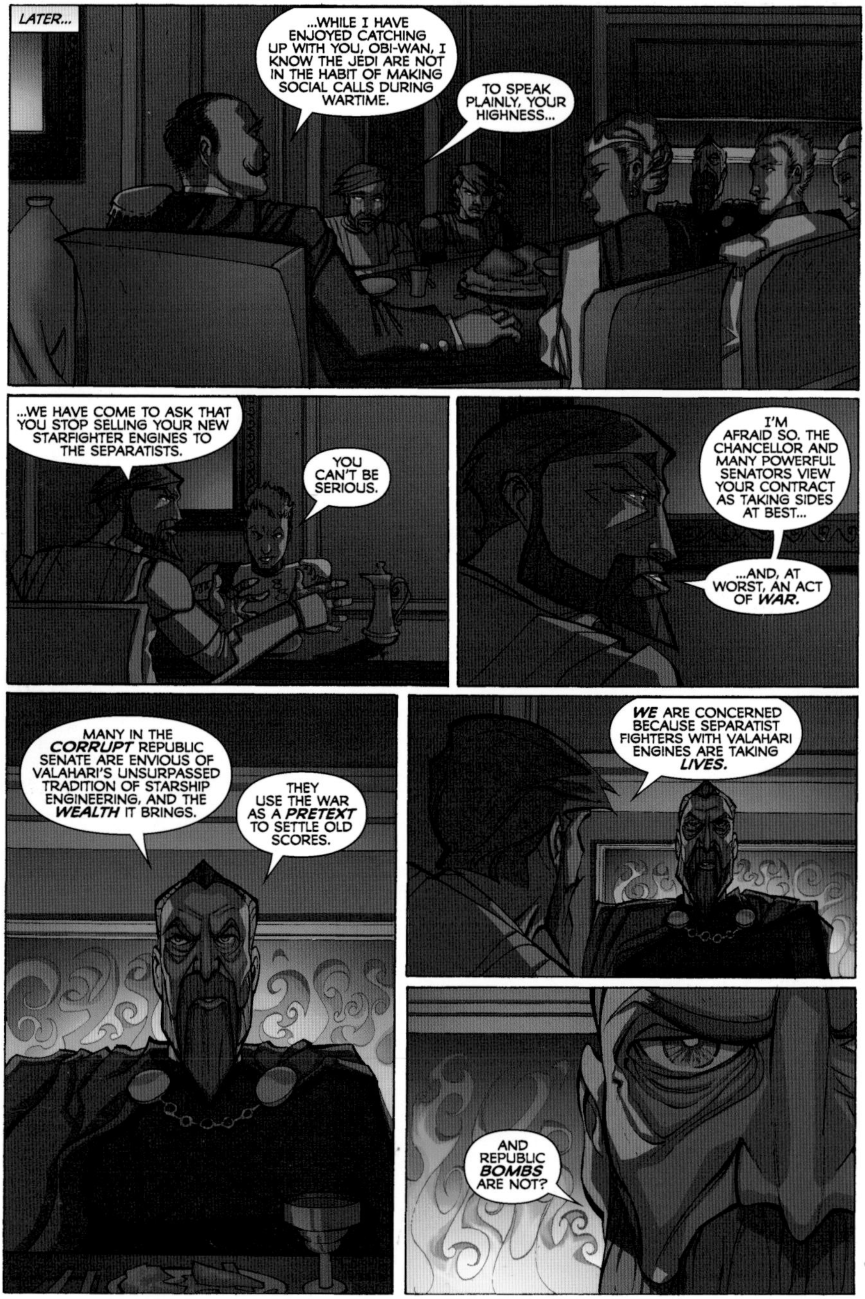
LATER...
...WHILE I HAVE ENJOYED CATCHING UP WITH YOU, OBI-WAN, I KNOW THE JEDI ARE NOT IN THE HABIT OF MAKING SOCIAL CALLS DURING WARTIME.
TO SPEAK PLAINLY, YOUR HIGHNESS...
...WE HAVE COME TO ASK THAT YOU STOP SELLING YOUR NEW STARFIGHTER ENGINES TO THE SEPARATISTS.
YOU CAN'T BE SERIOUS.
I'M AFRAID SO. THE CHANCELLOR AND MANY POWERFUL SENATORS VIEW YOUR CONTRACT AS TAKING SIDES AT BEST...
...AND, AT WORST, AN ACT OF WAR.
MANY IN THE CORRUPT REPUBLIC SENATE ARE ENVIOUS OF VALAHARI'S UNSURPASSED TRADITION OF STARSHIP ENGINEERING, AND THE WEALTH IT BRINGS.
THEY USE THE WAR AS A PRETEXT TO SETTLE OLD SCORES.
WE ARE CONCERNED BECAUSE SEPARATIST FIGHTERS WITH VALAHARI ENGINES ARE TAKING LIVES.
AND REPUBLIC BOMBS ARE NOT?

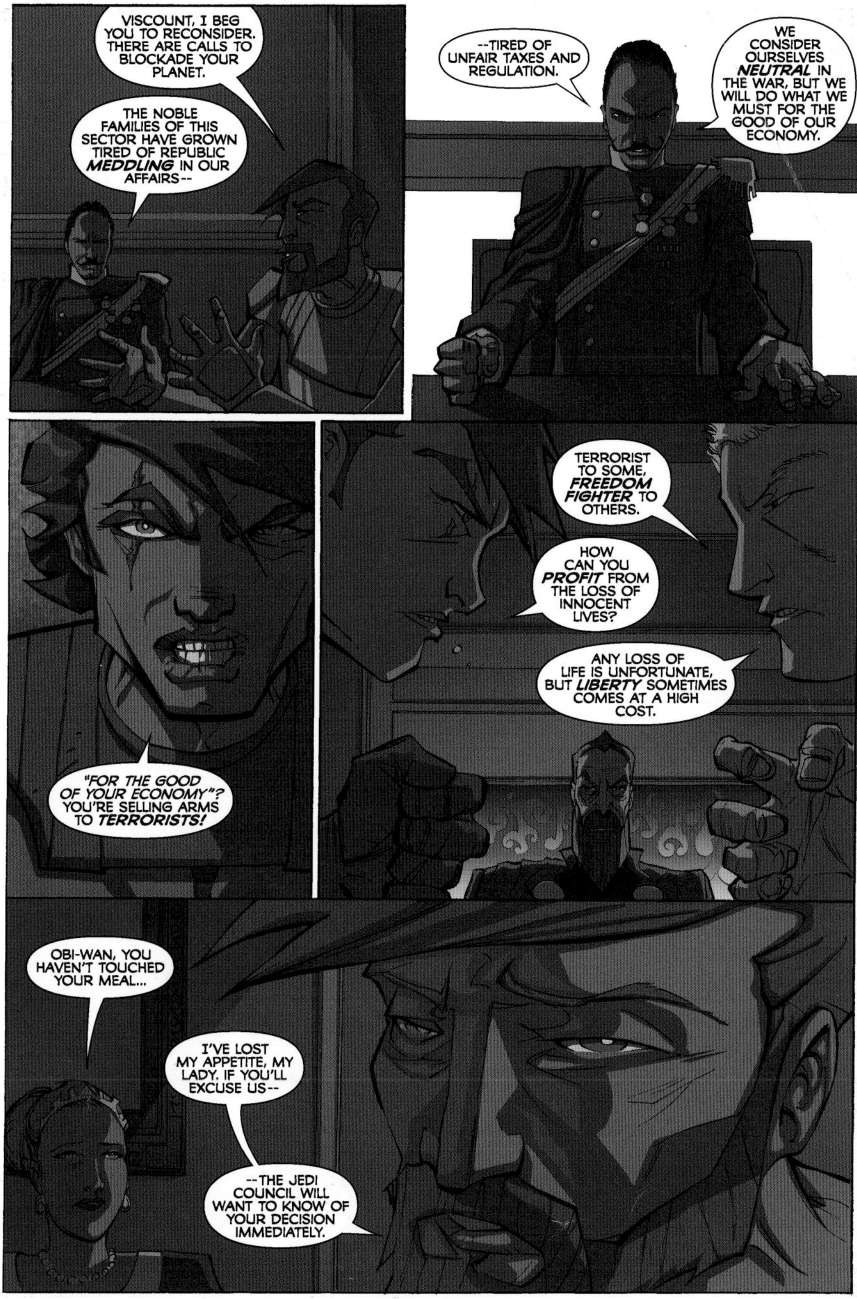
VISCOUNT, I BEG YOU TO RECONSIDER. THERE ARE CALLS TO BLOCKADE YOUR PLANET.
THE NOBLE FAMILIES OF THIS SECTOR HAVE GROWN TIRED OF REPUBLIC *MEDDLING* IN OUR AFFAIRS--
--TIRED OF UNFAIR TAXES AND REGULATION.
WE CONSIDER OURSELVES *NEUTRAL* IN THE WAR, BUT WE WILL DO WHAT WE MUST FOR THE GOOD OF OUR ECONOMY.
"FOR THE GOOD OF YOUR ECONOMY"? YOU'RE SELLING ARMS TO *TERRORISTS!*
TERRORIST TO SOME, *FREEDOM FIGHTER* TO OTHERS.
HOW CAN YOU *PROFIT* FROM THE LOSS OF INNOCENT LIVES?
ANY LOSS OF LIFE IS UNFORTUNATE, BUT *LIBERTY* SOMETIMES COMES AT A HIGH COST.
OBI-WAN, YOU HAVEN'T TOUCHED YOUR MEAL...
I'VE LOST MY APPETITE, MY LADY. IF YOU'LL EXCUSE US--
--THE JEDI COUNCIL WILL WANT TO KNOW OF YOUR DECISION IMMEDIATELY.

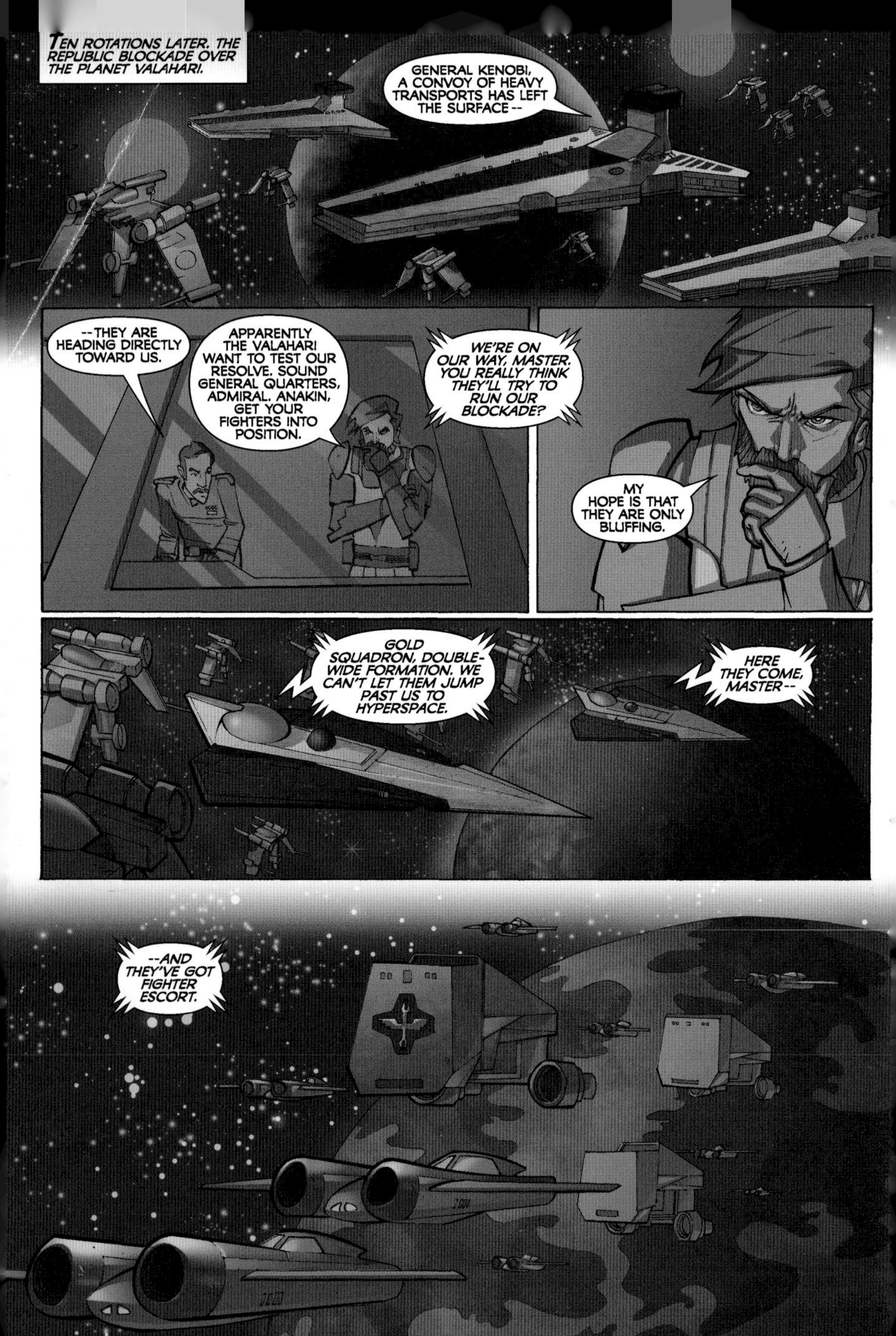
TEN ROTATIONS LATER. THE REPUBLIC BLOCKADE OVER THE PLANET VALAHARI.
GENERAL KENOBI, A CONVOY OF HEAVY TRANSPORTS HAS LEFT THE SURFACE--
--THEY ARE HEADING DIRECTLY TOWARD US.
APPARENTLY THE VALAHARI WANT TO TEST OUR RESOLVE. SOUND GENERAL QUARTERS, ADMIRAL. ANAKIN, GET YOUR FIGHTERS INTO POSITION.
WE'RE ON OUR WAY, MASTER. YOU REALLY THINK THEY'LL TRY TO RUN OUR BLOCKADE?
MY HOPE IS THAT THEY ARE ONLY BLUFFING.
GOLD SQUADRON, DOUBLE-WIDE FORMATION. WE CAN'T LET THEM JUMP PAST US TO HYPERSPACE.
HERE THEY COME, MASTER--
--AND THEY'VE GOT FIGHTER ESCORT.

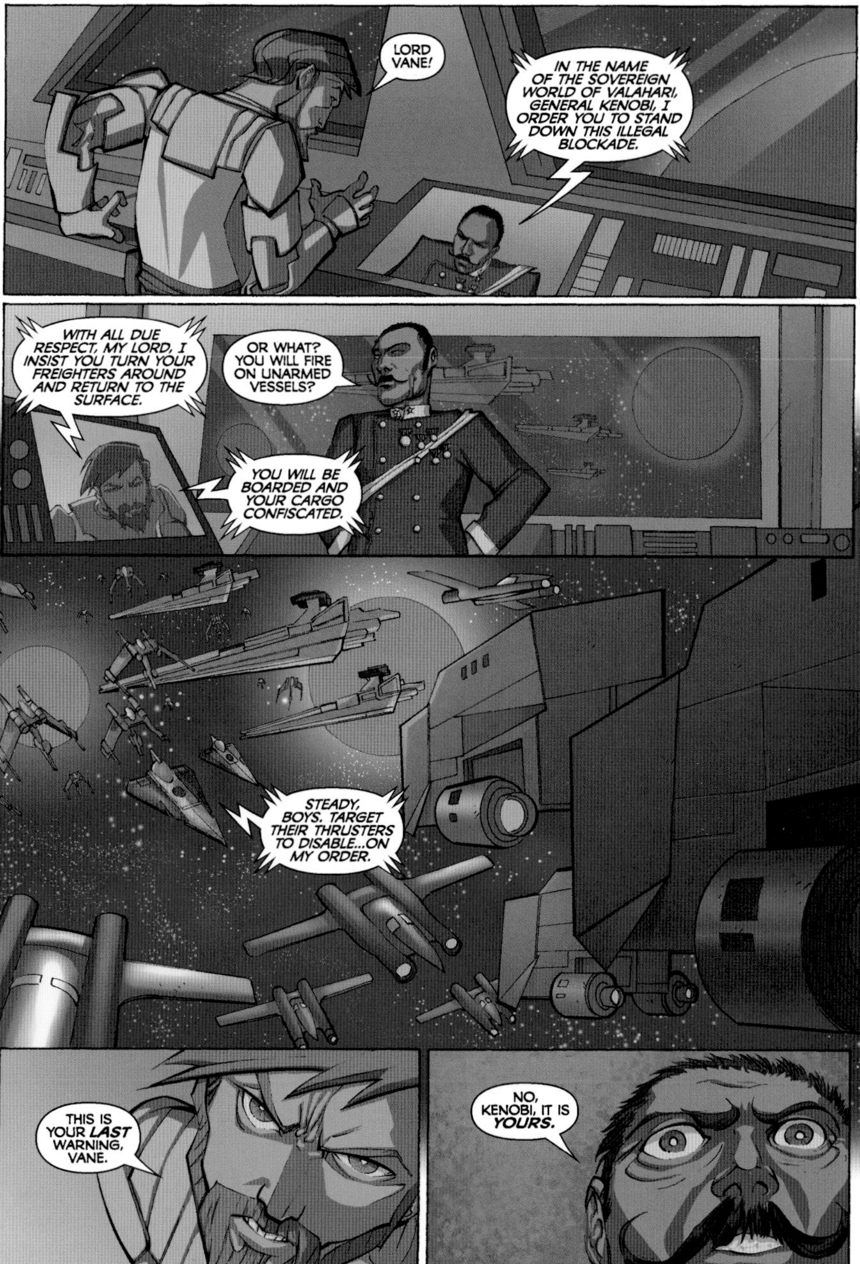
LORD VANE!
IN THE NAME OF THE SOVEREIGN WORLD OF VALAHARI, GENERAL KENOBI, I ORDER YOU TO STAND DOWN THIS ILLEGAL BLOCKADE.
WITH ALL DUE RESPECT, MY LORD, I INSIST YOU TURN YOUR FREIGHTERS AROUND AND RETURN TO THE SURFACE.
OR WHAT? YOU WILL FIRE ON UNARMED VESSELS?
YOU WILL BE BOARDED AND YOUR CARGO CONFISCATED.
STEADY, BOYS. TARGET THEIR THRUSTERS TO DISABLE...ON MY ORDER.
THIS IS YOUR LAST WARNING, VANE.
NO, KENOBI, IT IS YOURS.

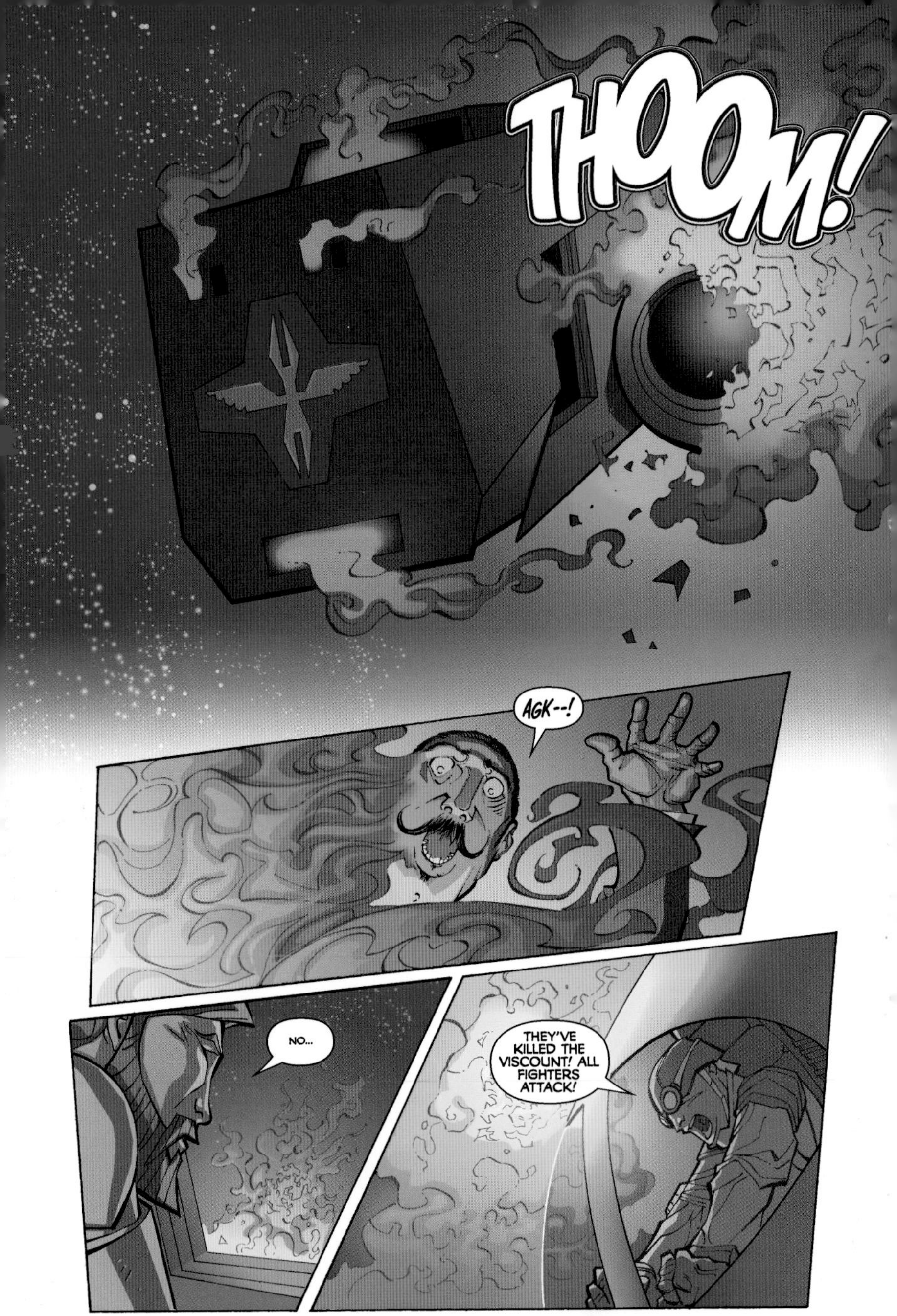
THOOM!
AGK--!
NO...
THEY'VE KILLED THE VISCOUNT! ALL FIGHTERS ATTACK!

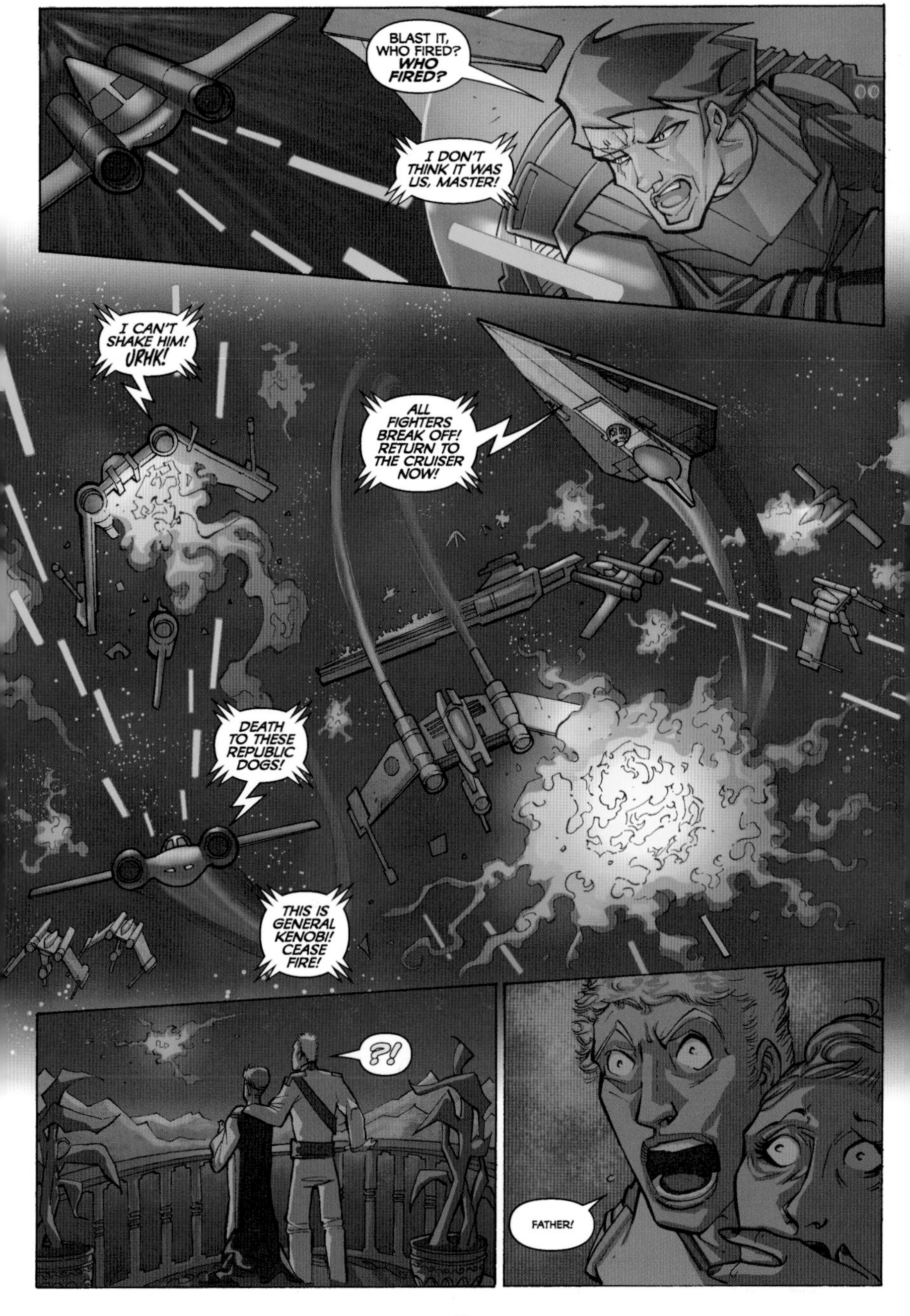
BLAST IT, WHO FIRED? WHO FIRED?
I DON'T THINK IT WAS US, MASTER!
I CAN'T SHAKE HIM! URHK!
ALL FIGHTERS BREAK OFF! RETURN TO THE CRUISER NOW!
DEATH TO THESE REPUBLIC DOGS!
THIS IS GENERAL KENOBI! CEASE FIRE!
?!
FATHER!

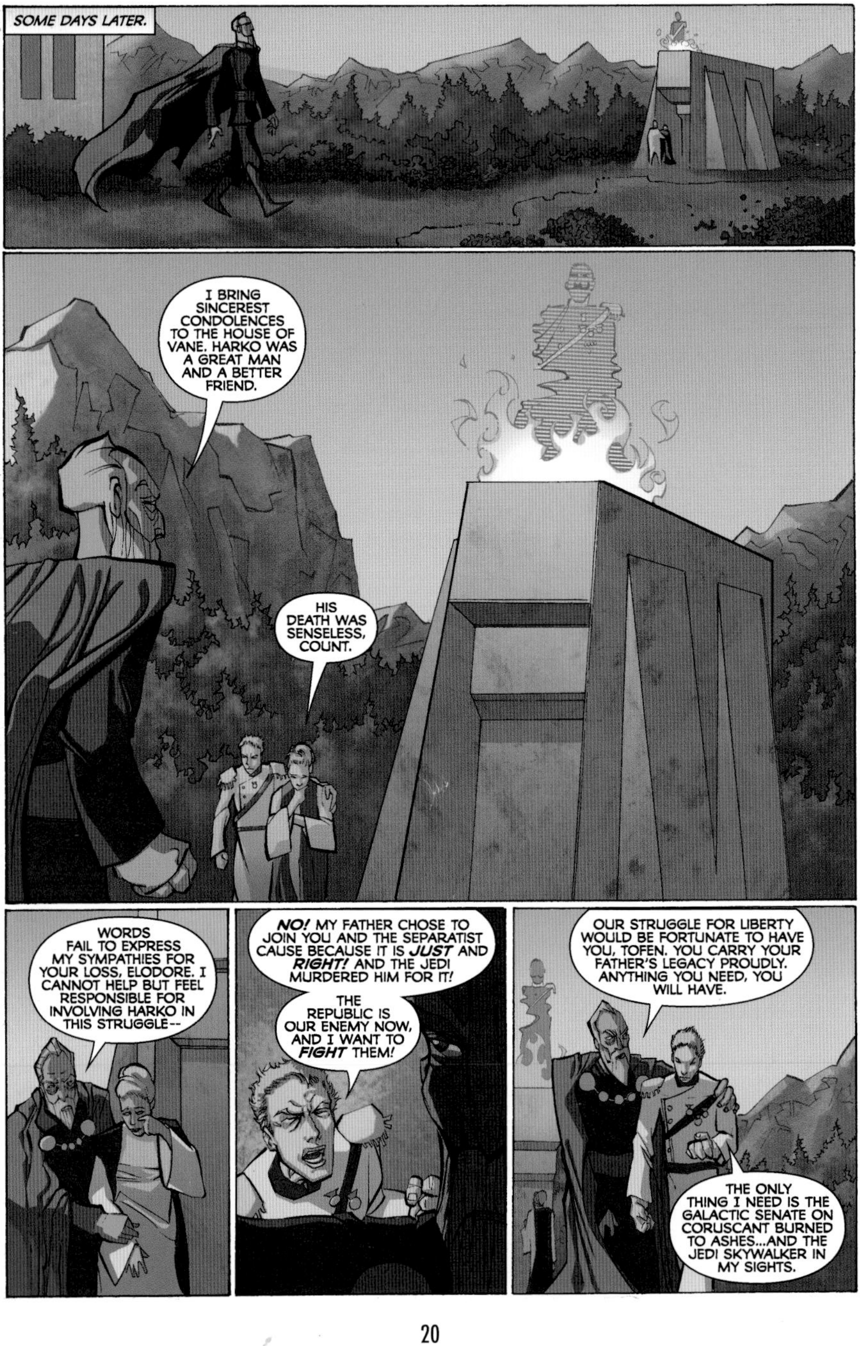
SOME DAYS LATER.
I BRING SINCEREST CONDOLENCES TO THE HOUSE OF VANE. HARKO WAS A GREAT MAN AND A BETTER FRIEND.
HIS DEATH WAS SENSELESS, COUNT.
WORDS FAIL TO EXPRESS MY SYMPATHIES FOR YOUR LOSS, ELODORE. I CANNOT HELP BUT FEEL RESPONSIBLE FOR INVOLVING HARKO IN THIS STRUGGLE--
NO! MY FATHER CHOSE TO JOIN YOU AND THE SEPARATIST CAUSE BECAUSE IT IS JUST AND RIGHT! AND THE JEDI MURDERED HIM FOR IT!
THE REPUBLIC IS OUR ENEMY NOW, AND I WANT TO FIGHT THEM!
OUR STRUGGLE FOR LIBERTY WOULD BE FORTUNATE TO HAVE YOU, TOFEN. YOU CARRY YOUR FATHER'S LEGACY PROUDLY. ANYTHING YOU NEED, YOU WILL HAVE.
THE ONLY THING I NEED IS THE GALACTIC SENATE ON CORUSCANT BURNED TO ASHES...AND THE JEDI SKYWALKER IN MY SIGHTS.

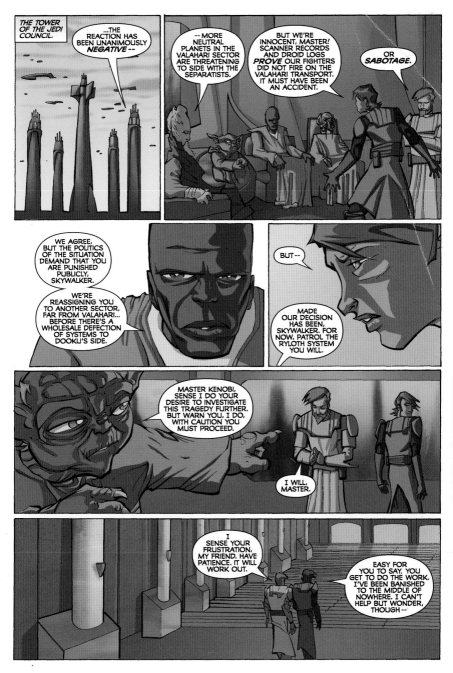

THE TOWER OF THE JEDI COUNCIL.

...THE REACTION HAS BEEN UNANIMOUSLY *NEGATIVE* --

-- MORE NEUTRAL PLANETS IN THE VALAHARI SECTOR ARE THREATENING TO SIDE WITH THE SEPARATISTS.

BUT WE'RE INNOCENT, MASTER! SCANNER RECORDS AND DROID LOGS *PROVE* OUR FIGHTERS DID NOT FIRE ON THE VALAHARI TRANSPORT. IT MUST HAVE BEEN AN ACCIDENT.

OR *SABOTAGE*.

WE AGREE, BUT THE POLITICS OF THE SITUATION DEMAND THAT YOU ARE PUNISHED PUBLICLY, SKYWALKER.

WE'RE REASSIGNING YOU TO ANOTHER SECTOR... FAR FROM VALAHARI... BEFORE THERE'S A WHOLESALE DEFECTION OF SYSTEMS TO DOOKU'S SIDE.

BUT --

MADE OUR DECISION HAS BEEN, SKYWALKER. FOR NOW, PATROL THE RYLOTH SYSTEM YOU WILL.

MASTER KENOBI, SENSE I DO YOUR DESIRE TO INVESTIGATE THIS TRAGEDY FURTHER. BUT WARN YOU, I DO, WITH CAUTION YOU MUST PROCEED.

I WILL, MASTER.

I SENSE YOUR FRUSTRATION, MY FRIEND. HAVE PATIENCE. IT WILL WORK OUT.

EASY FOR YOU TO SAY. YOU GET TO DO THE WORK. I'VE BEEN BANISHED TO THE MIDDLE OF NOWHERE. I CAN'T HELP BUT WONDER, THOUGH --

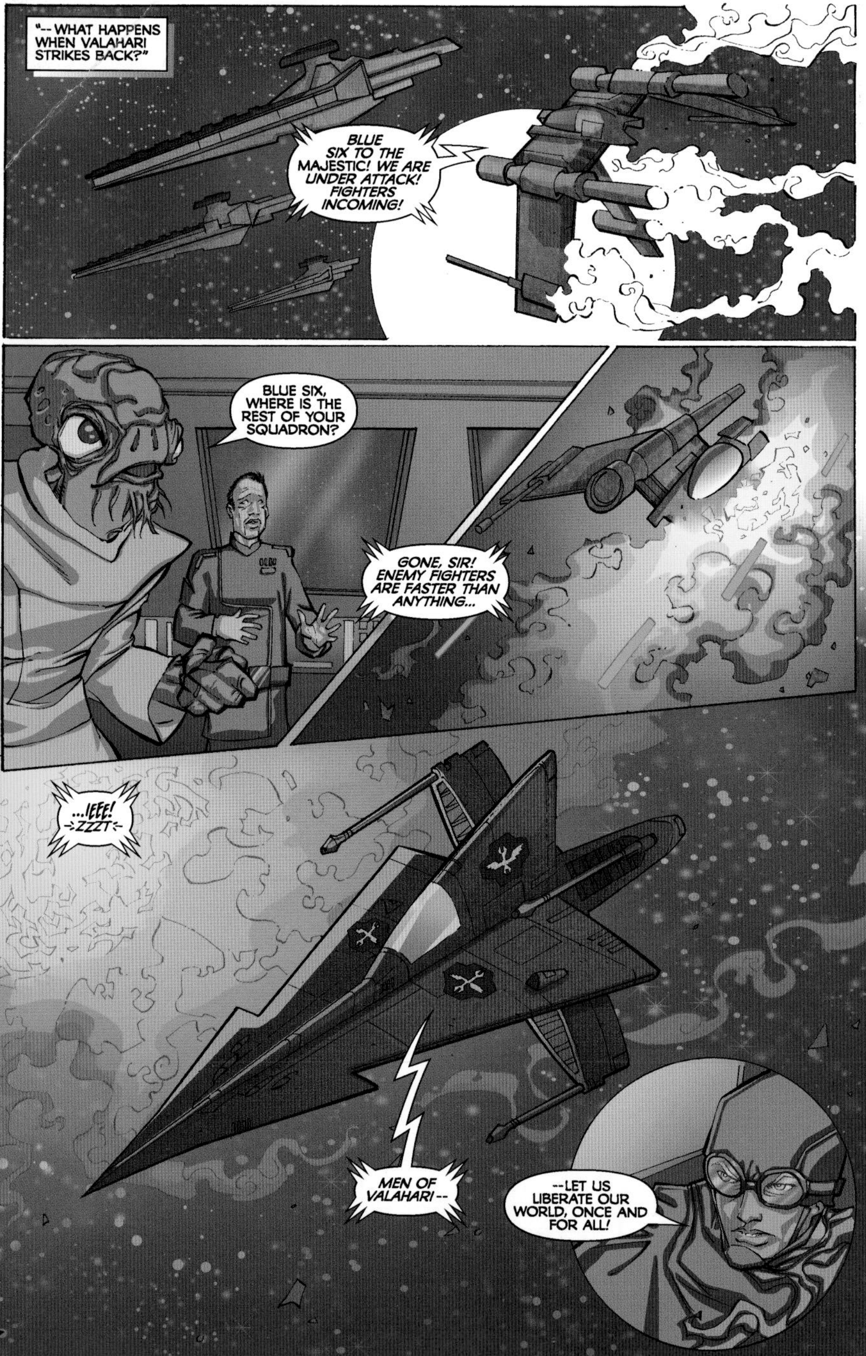
"-- WHAT HAPPENS WHEN VALAHARI STRIKES BACK?"
BLUE SIX TO THE MAJESTIC! WE ARE UNDER ATTACK! FIGHTERS INCOMING!
BLUE SIX, WHERE IS THE REST OF YOUR SQUADRON?
GONE, SIR! ENEMY FIGHTERS ARE FASTER THAN ANYTHING...
...IEEE! -ZZZT-
MEN OF VALAHARI --
--LET US LIBERATE OUR WORLD, ONCE AND FOR ALL!

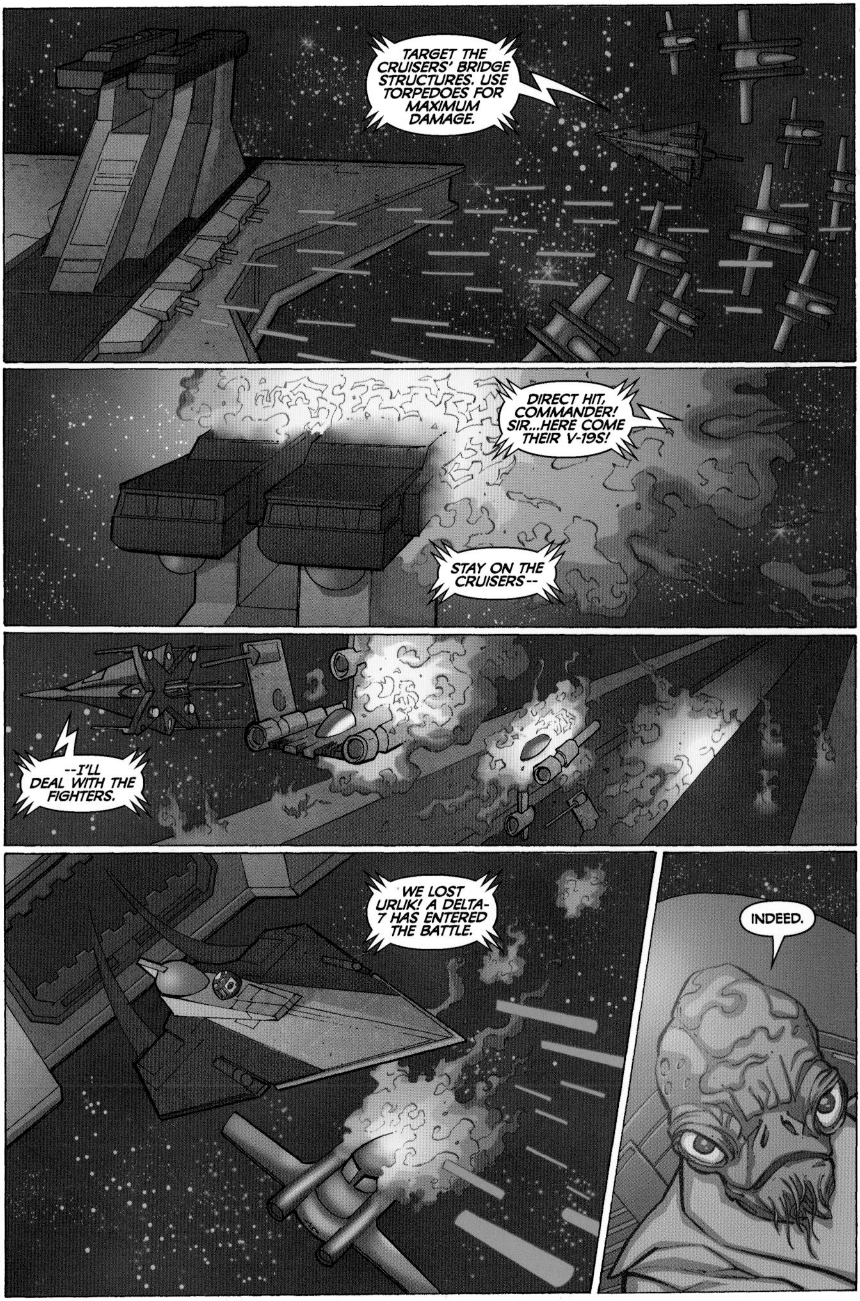
TARGET THE CRUISERS' BRIDGE STRUCTURES. USE TORPEDOES FOR MAXIMUM DAMAGE.
DIRECT HIT, COMMANDER! SIR...HERE COME THEIR V-19S!
STAY ON THE CRUISERS--
--I'LL DEAL WITH THE FIGHTERS.
WE LOST URLIK! A DELTA-7 HAS ENTERED THE BATTLE.
INDEED.

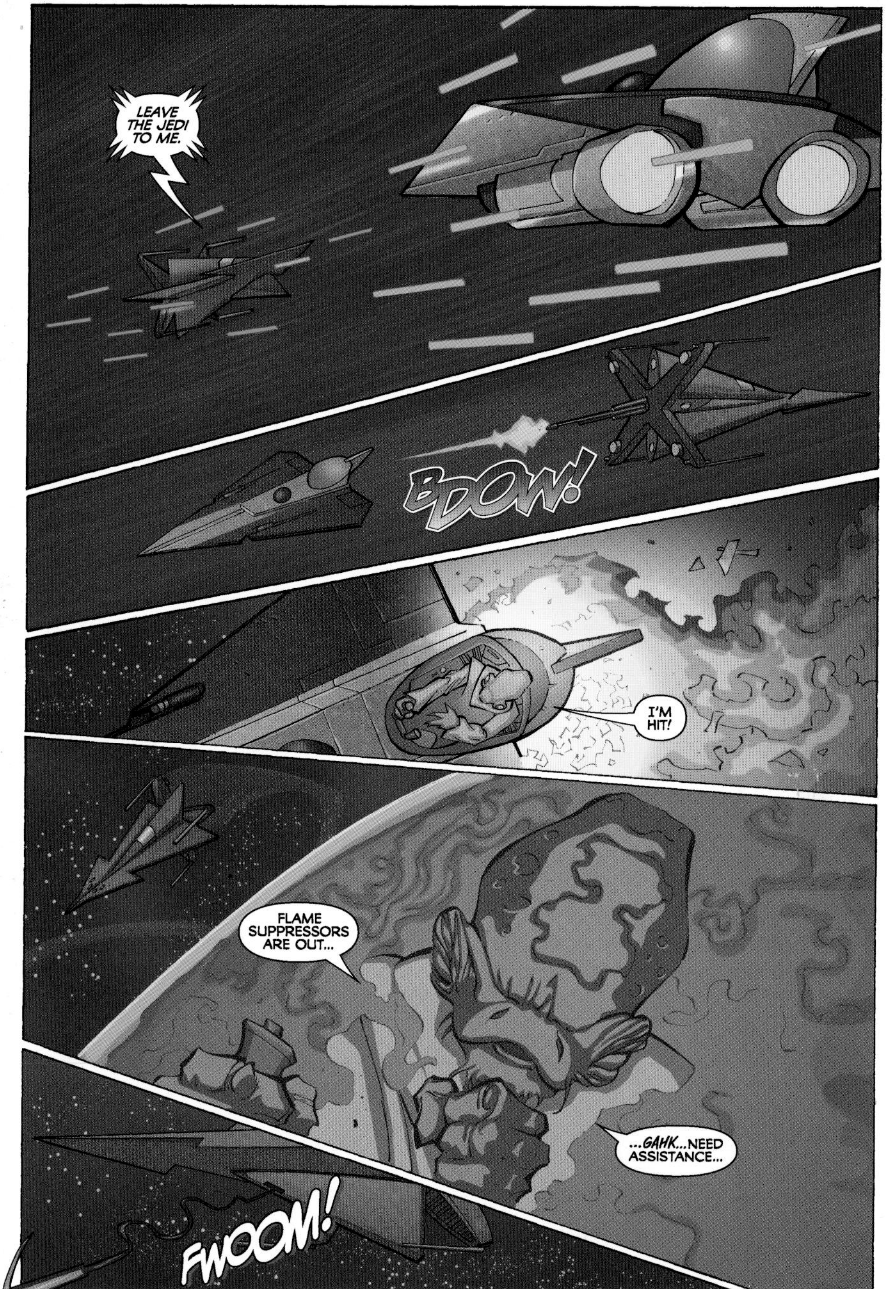

LEAVE THE JEDI TO ME.
BDOW!
I'M HIT!
FLAME SUPPRESSORS ARE OUT...
...GAHK...NEED ASSISTANCE...
FWOOM!

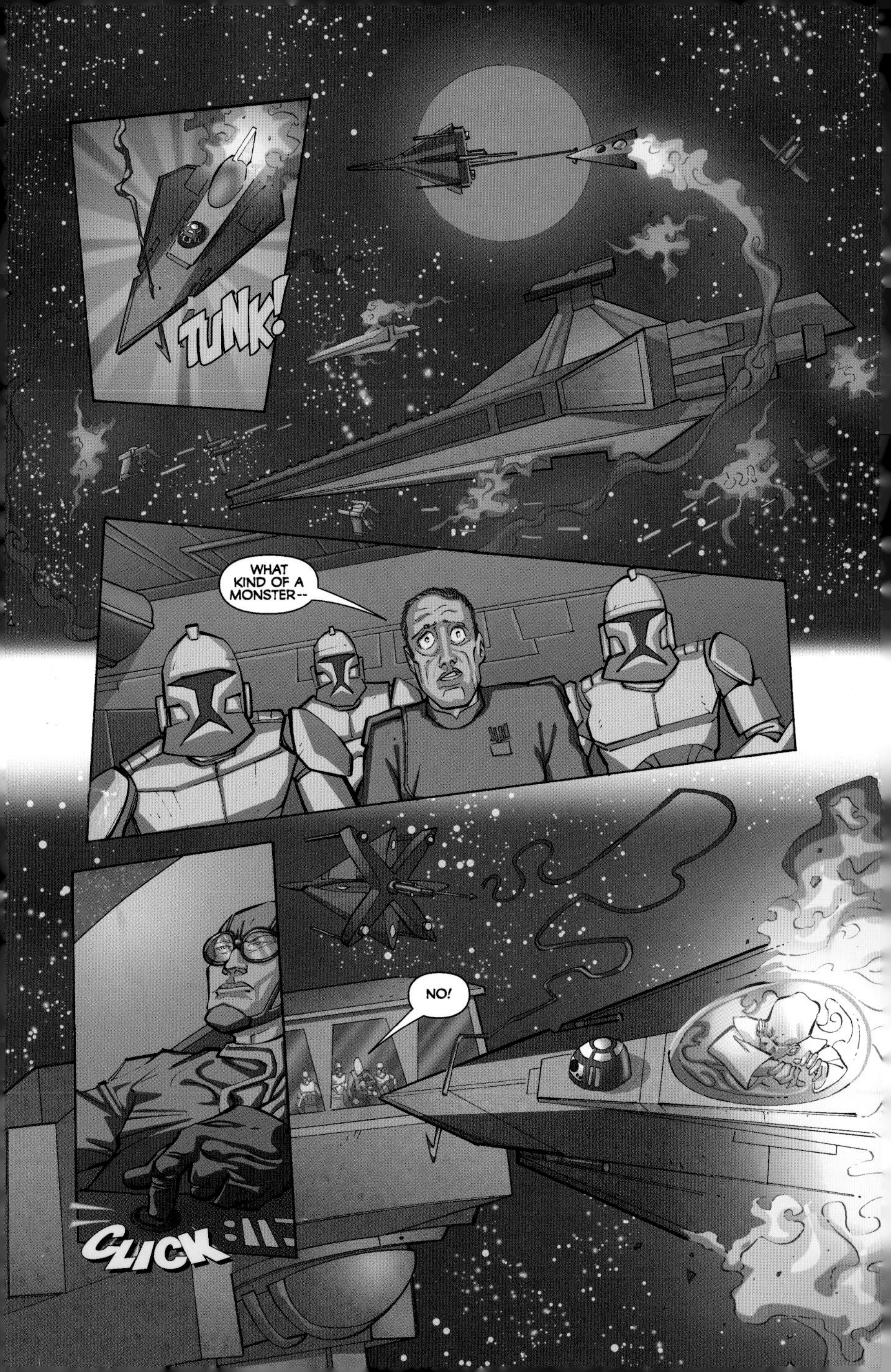
TUNK!
WHAT KIND OF A MONSTER--
NO!
CLICK

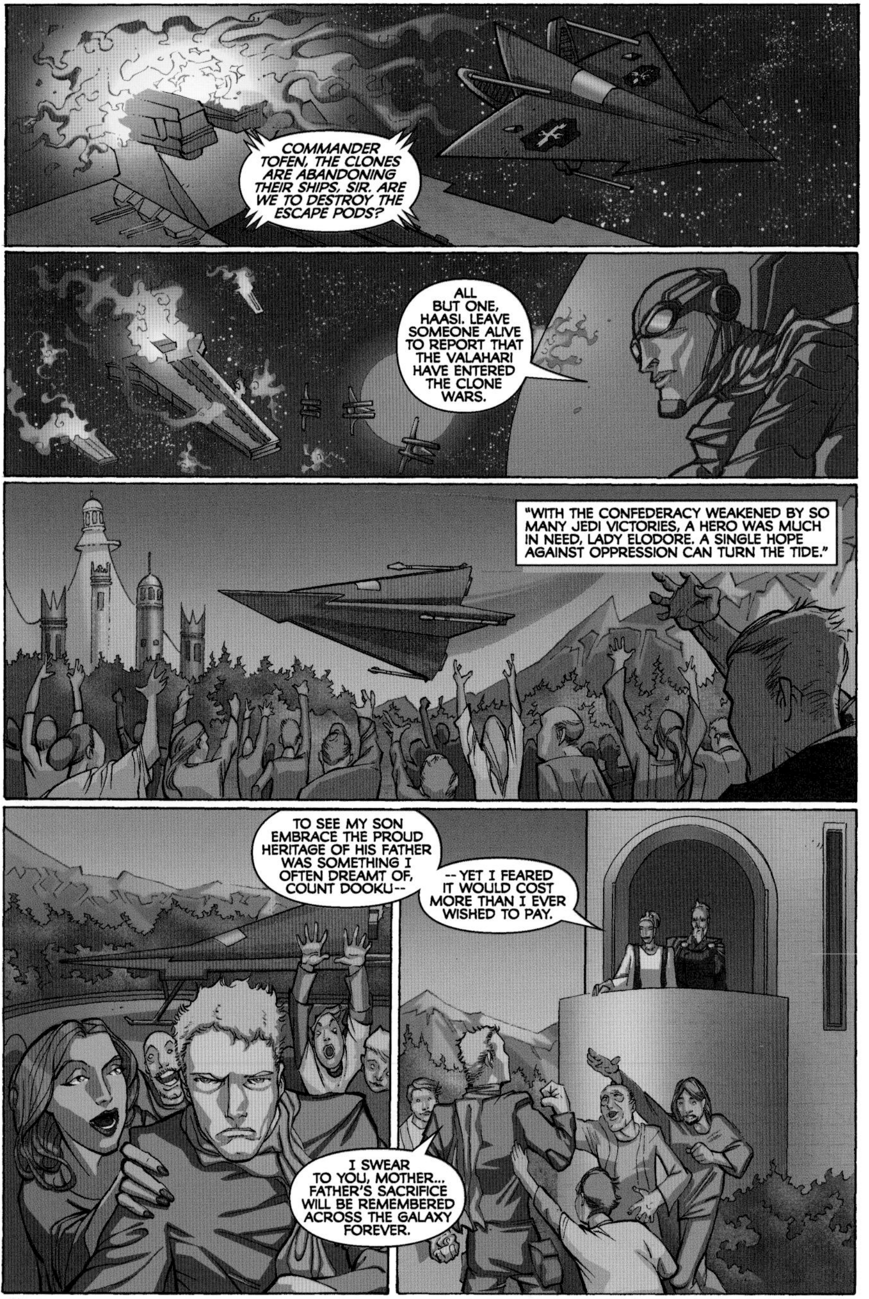
COMMANDER TOFEN, THE CLONES ARE ABANDONING THEIR SHIPS, SIR. ARE WE TO DESTROY THE ESCAPE PODS?
ALL BUT ONE, HAASI. LEAVE SOMEONE ALIVE TO REPORT THAT THE VALAHARI HAVE ENTERED THE CLONE WARS.
"WITH THE CONFEDERACY WEAKENED BY SO MANY JEDI VICTORIES, A HERO WAS MUCH IN NEED, LADY ELODORE. A SINGLE HOPE AGAINST OPPRESSION CAN TURN THE TIDE."
TO SEE MY SON EMBRACE THE PROUD HERITAGE OF HIS FATHER WAS SOMETHING I OFTEN DREAMT OF, COUNT DOOKU--
--YET I FEARED IT WOULD COST MORE THAN I EVER WISHED TO PAY.
I SWEAR TO YOU, MOTHER... FATHER'S SACRIFICE WILL BE REMEMBERED ACROSS THE GALAXY FOREVER.

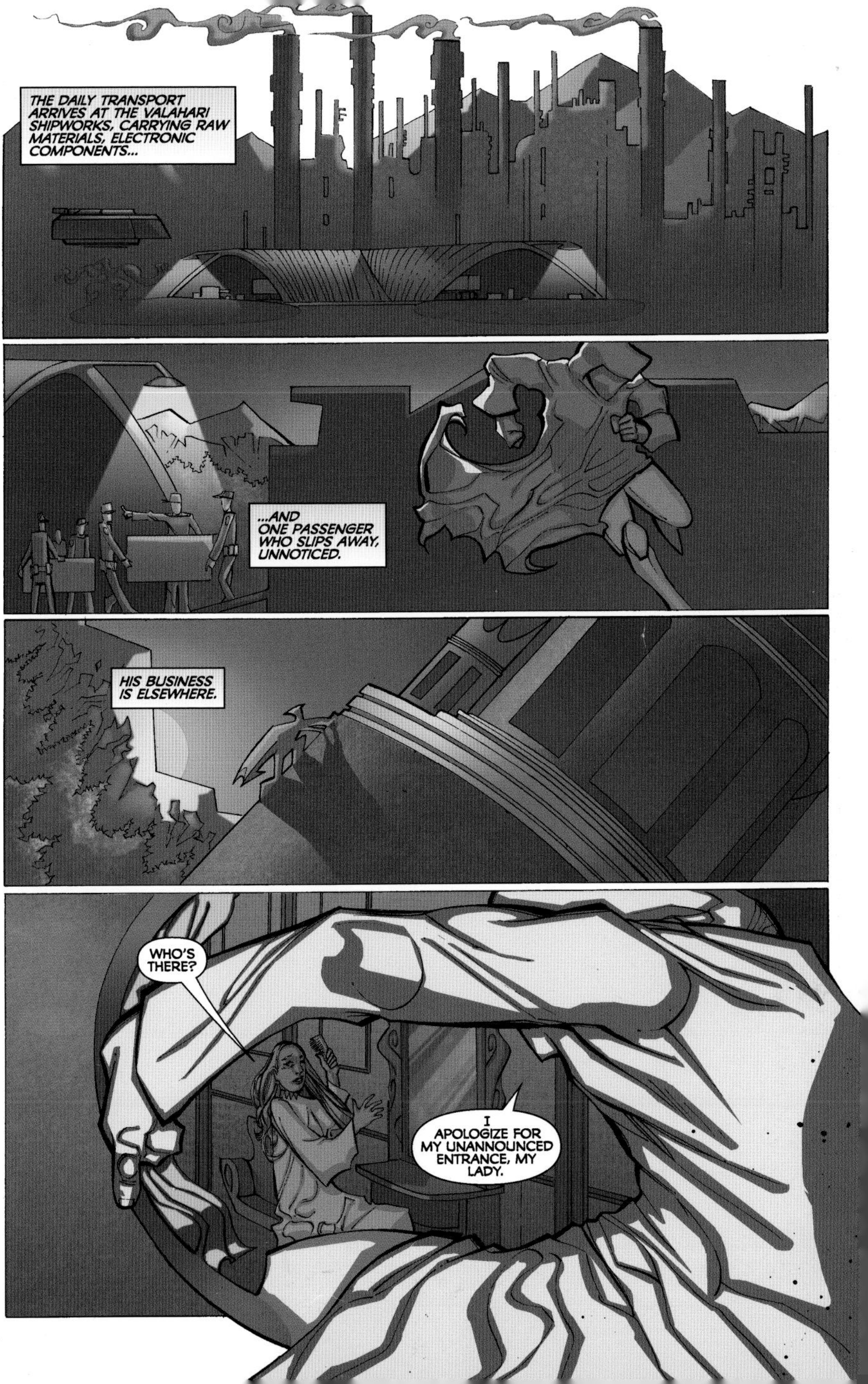
THE DAILY TRANSPORT ARRIVES AT THE VALAHARI SHIPWORKS, CARRYING RAW MATERIALS, ELECTRONIC COMPONENTS...
...AND ONE PASSENGER WHO SLIPS AWAY, UNNOTICED.
HIS BUSINESS IS ELSEWHERE.
WHO'S THERE?
I APOLOGIZE FOR MY UNANNOUNCED ENTRANCE, MY LADY.

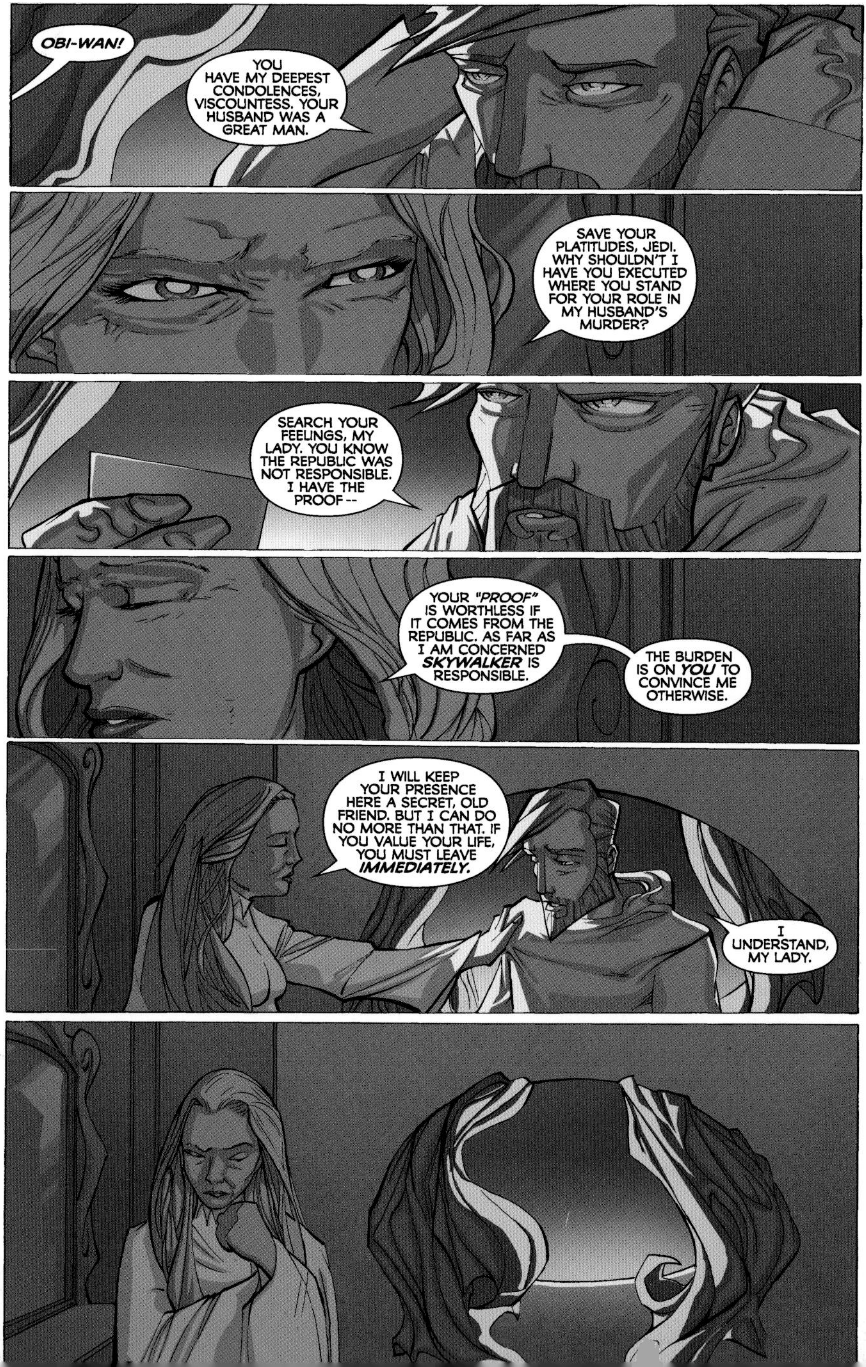
OBI-WAN!
YOU HAVE MY DEEPEST CONDOLENCES, VISCOUNTESS. YOUR HUSBAND WAS A GREAT MAN.
SAVE YOUR PLATITUDES, JEDI. WHY SHOULDN'T I HAVE YOU EXECUTED WHERE YOU STAND FOR YOUR ROLE IN MY HUSBAND'S MURDER?
SEARCH YOUR FEELINGS, MY LADY. YOU KNOW THE REPUBLIC WAS NOT RESPONSIBLE. I HAVE THE PROOF--
YOUR "PROOF" IS WORTHLESS IF IT COMES FROM THE REPUBLIC. AS FAR AS I AM CONCERNED SKYWALKER IS RESPONSIBLE.
THE BURDEN IS ON YOU TO CONVINCE ME OTHERWISE.
I WILL KEEP YOUR PRESENCE HERE A SECRET, OLD FRIEND. BUT I CAN DO NO MORE THAN THAT. IF YOU VALUE YOUR LIFE, YOU MUST LEAVE IMMEDIATELY.
I UNDERSTAND, MY LADY.

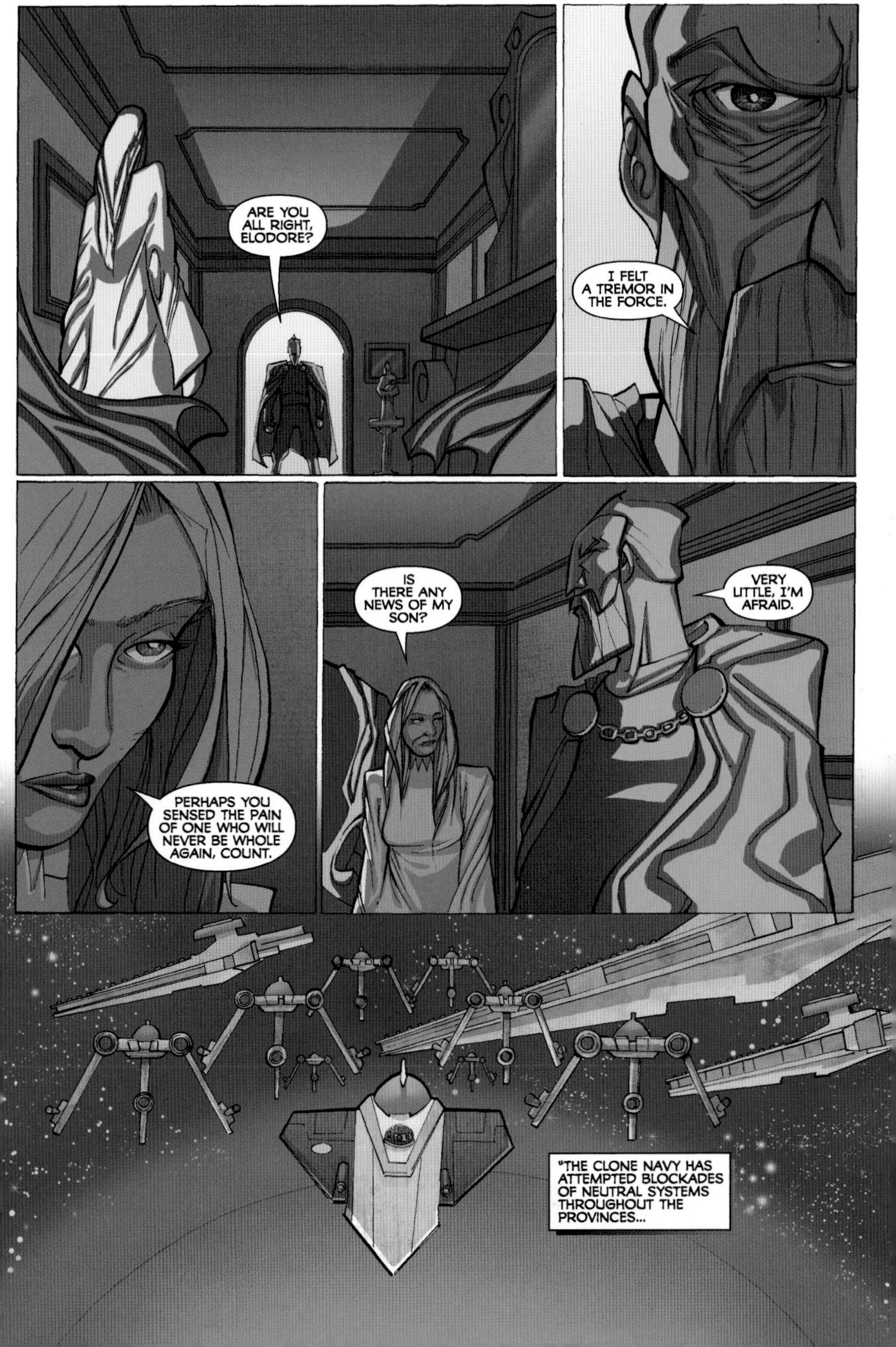
ARE YOU ALL RIGHT, ELODORE?
I FELT A TREMOR IN THE FORCE.
PERHAPS YOU SENSED THE PAIN OF ONE WHO WILL NEVER BE WHOLE AGAIN, COUNT.
IS THERE ANY NEWS OF MY SON?
VERY LITTLE, I'M AFRAID.
"THE CLONE NAVY HAS ATTEMPTED BLOCKADES OF NEUTRAL SYSTEMS THROUGHOUT THE PROVINCES...

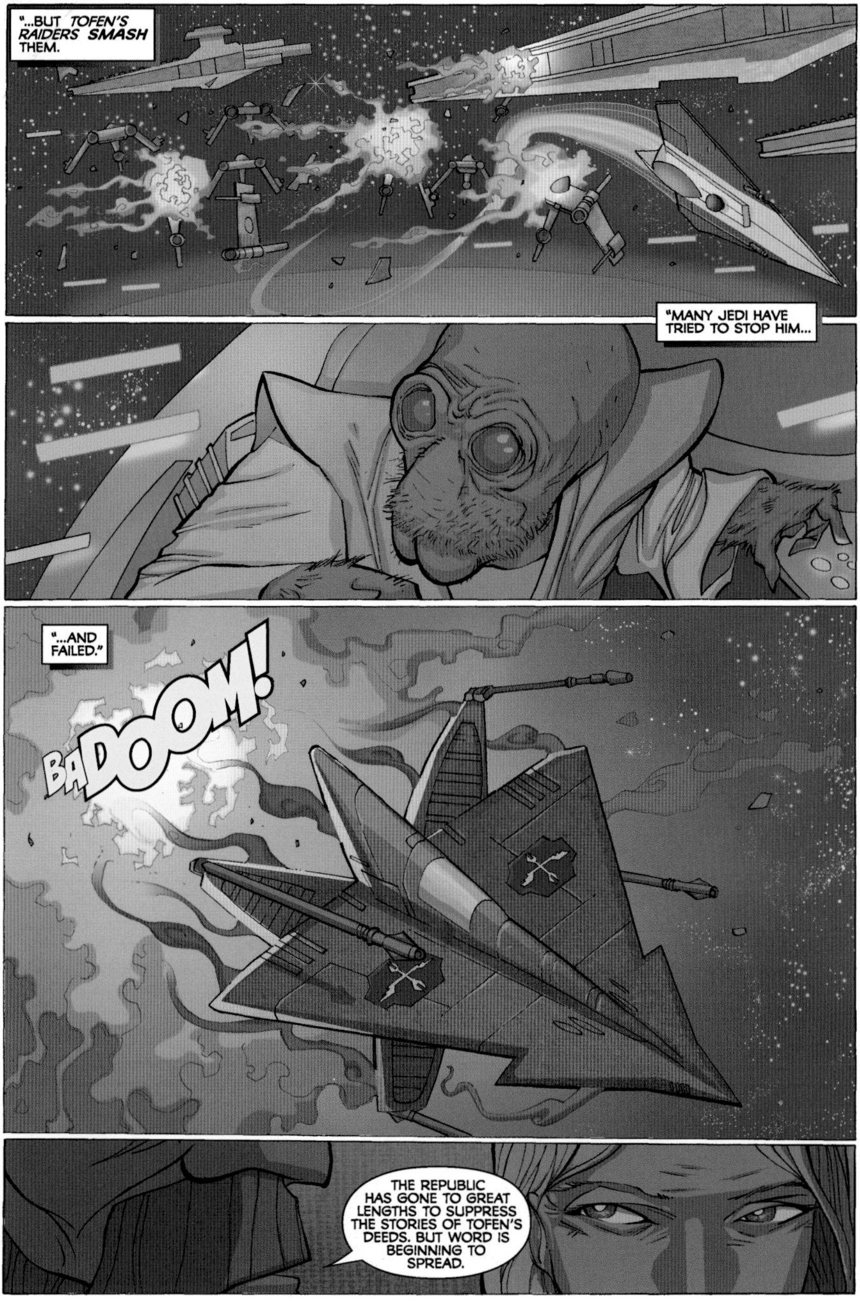
"...BUT TOFEN'S RAIDERS SMASH THEM.
"MANY JEDI HAVE TRIED TO STOP HIM...
"...AND FAILED."
BADOOOM!
THE REPUBLIC HAS GONE TO GREAT LENGTHS TO SUPPRESS THE STORIES OF TOFEN'S DEEDS. BUT WORD IS BEGINNING TO SPREAD.

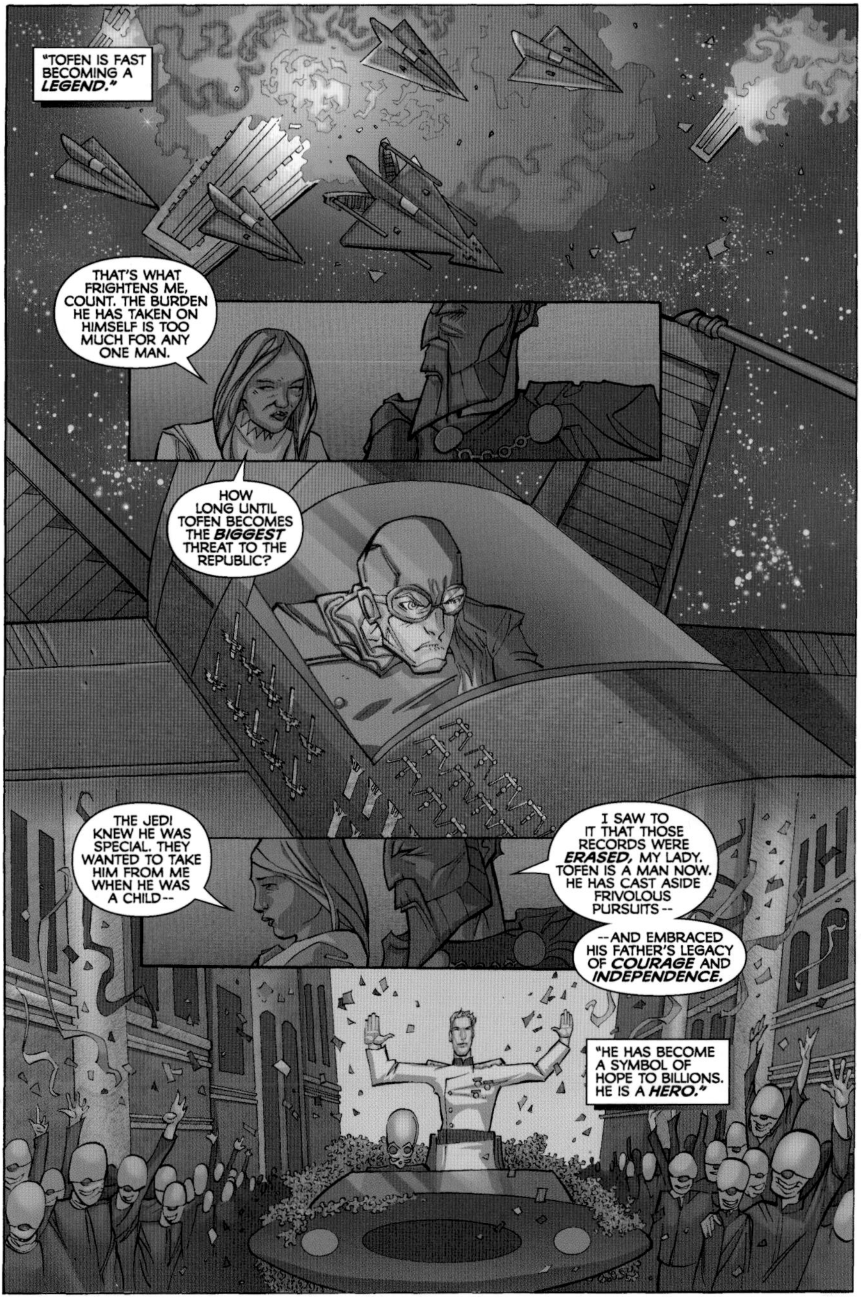
"TOFEN IS FAST BECOMING A LEGEND."
THAT'S WHAT FRIGHTENS ME, COUNT. THE BURDEN HE HAS TAKEN ON HIMSELF IS TOO MUCH FOR ANY ONE MAN.
HOW LONG UNTIL TOFEN BECOMES THE BIGGEST THREAT TO THE REPUBLIC?
THE JEDI KNEW HE WAS SPECIAL. THEY WANTED TO TAKE HIM FROM ME WHEN HE WAS A CHILD--
I SAW TO IT THAT THOSE RECORDS WERE ERASED, MY LADY. TOFEN IS A MAN NOW. HE HAS CAST ASIDE FRIVOLOUS PURSUITS--
--AND EMBRACED HIS FATHER'S LEGACY OF COURAGE AND INDEPENDENCE.
"HE HAS BECOME A SYMBOL OF HOPE TO BILLIONS. HE IS A HERO."

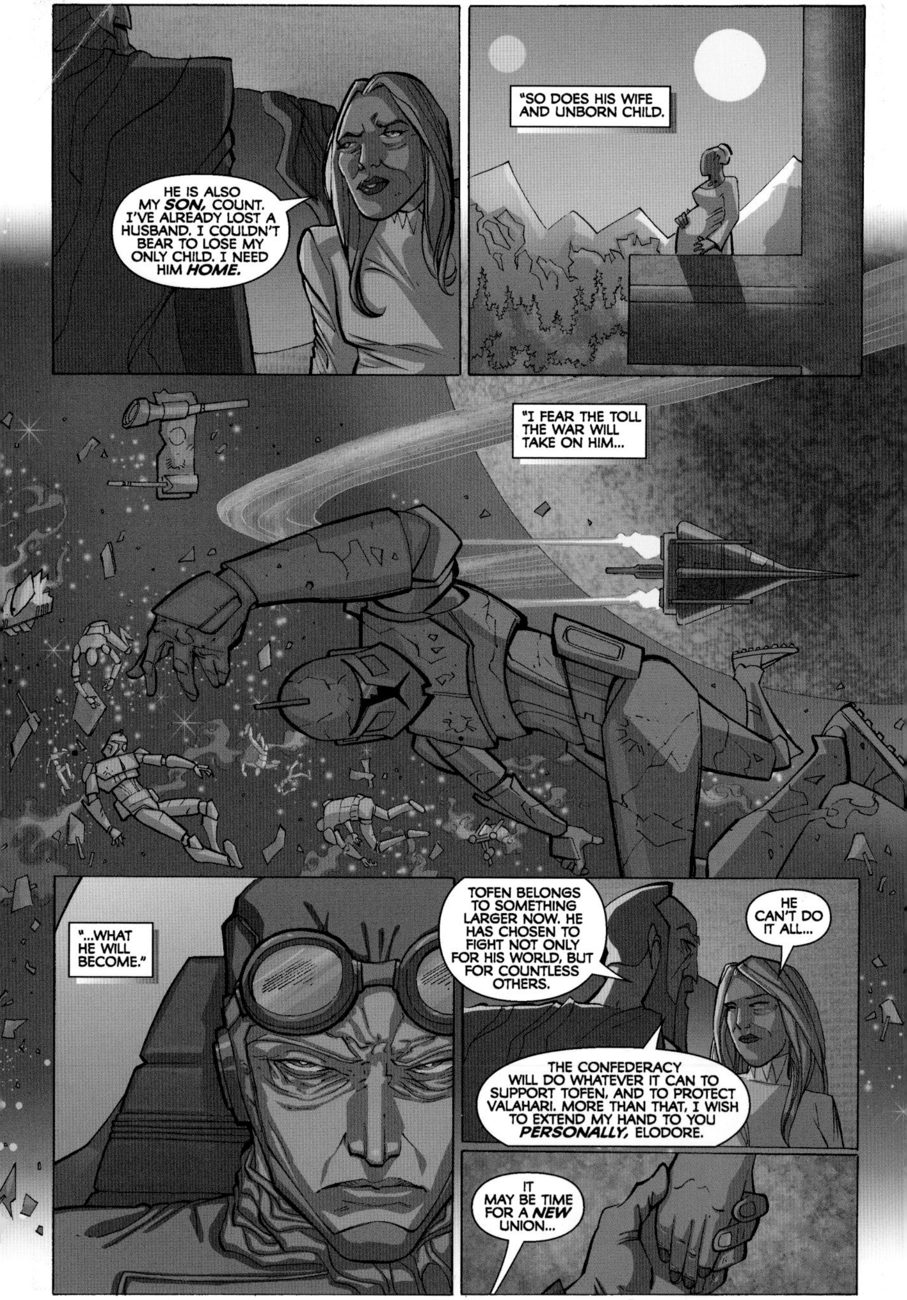
HE IS ALSO MY SON, COUNT. I'VE ALREADY LOST A HUSBAND. I COULDN'T BEAR TO LOSE MY ONLY CHILD. I NEED HIM HOME.
"SO DOES HIS WIFE AND UNBORN CHILD.
"I FEAR THE TOLL THE WAR WILL TAKE ON HIM...
"...WHAT HE WILL BECOME."
TOFEN BELONGS TO SOMETHING LARGER NOW. HE HAS CHOSEN TO FIGHT NOT ONLY FOR HIS WORLD, BUT FOR COUNTLESS OTHERS.
HE CAN'T DO IT ALL...
THE CONFEDERACY WILL DO WHATEVER IT CAN TO SUPPORT TOFEN, AND TO PROTECT VALAHARI. MORE THAN THAT, I WISH TO EXTEND MY HAND TO YOU PERSONALLY, ELODORE.
IT MAY BE TIME FOR A NEW UNION...

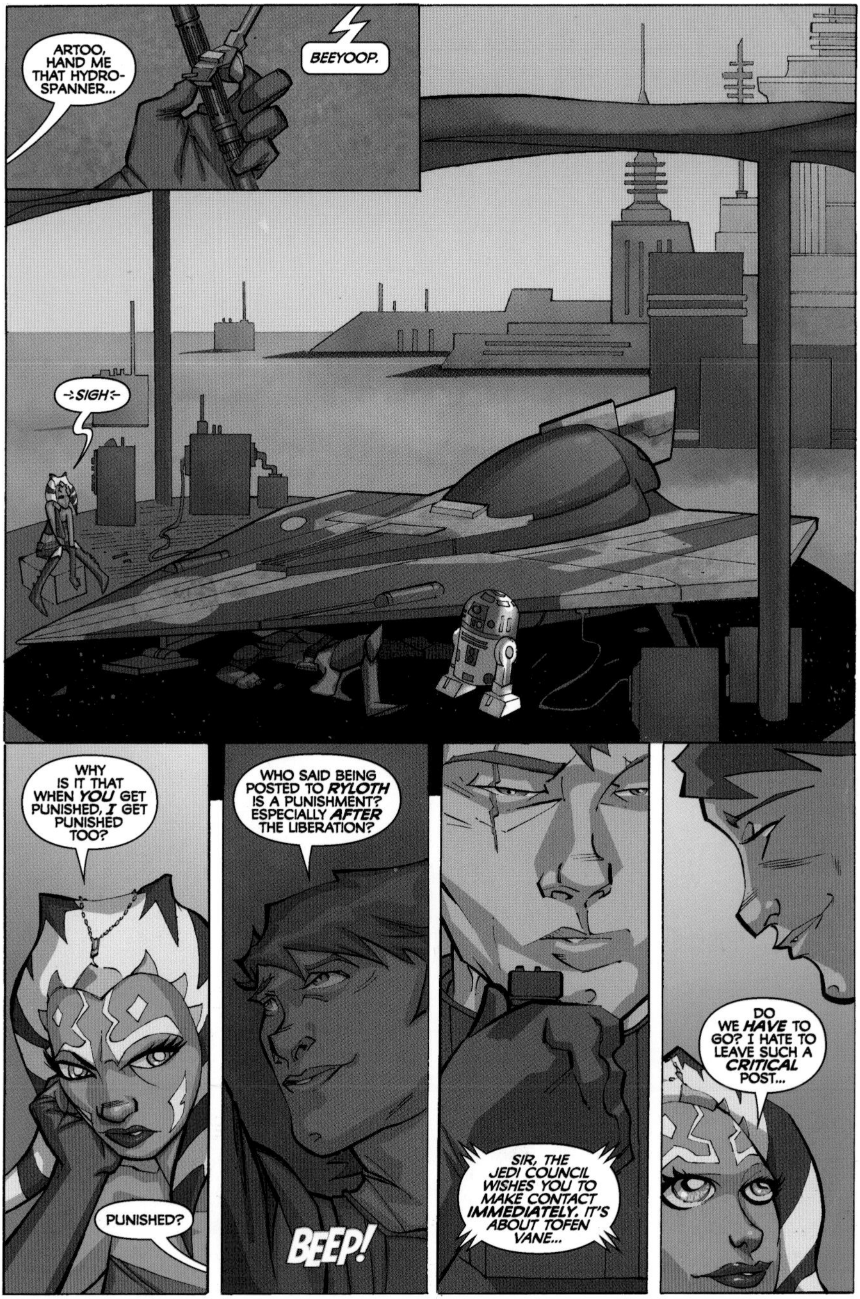
ARTOO, HAND ME THAT HYDRO-SPANNER...
BEEYOOP.
-SIGH-
WHY IS IT THAT WHEN YOU GET PUNISHED, I GET PUNISHED TOO?
PUNISHED?
WHO SAID BEING POSTED TO RYLOTH IS A PUNISHMENT? ESPECIALLY AFTER THE LIBERATION?
BEEP!
SIR, THE JEDI COUNCIL WISHES YOU TO MAKE CONTACT IMMEDIATELY. IT'S ABOUT TOFEN VANE...
DO WE HAVE TO GO? I HATE TO LEAVE SUCH A CRITICAL POST...

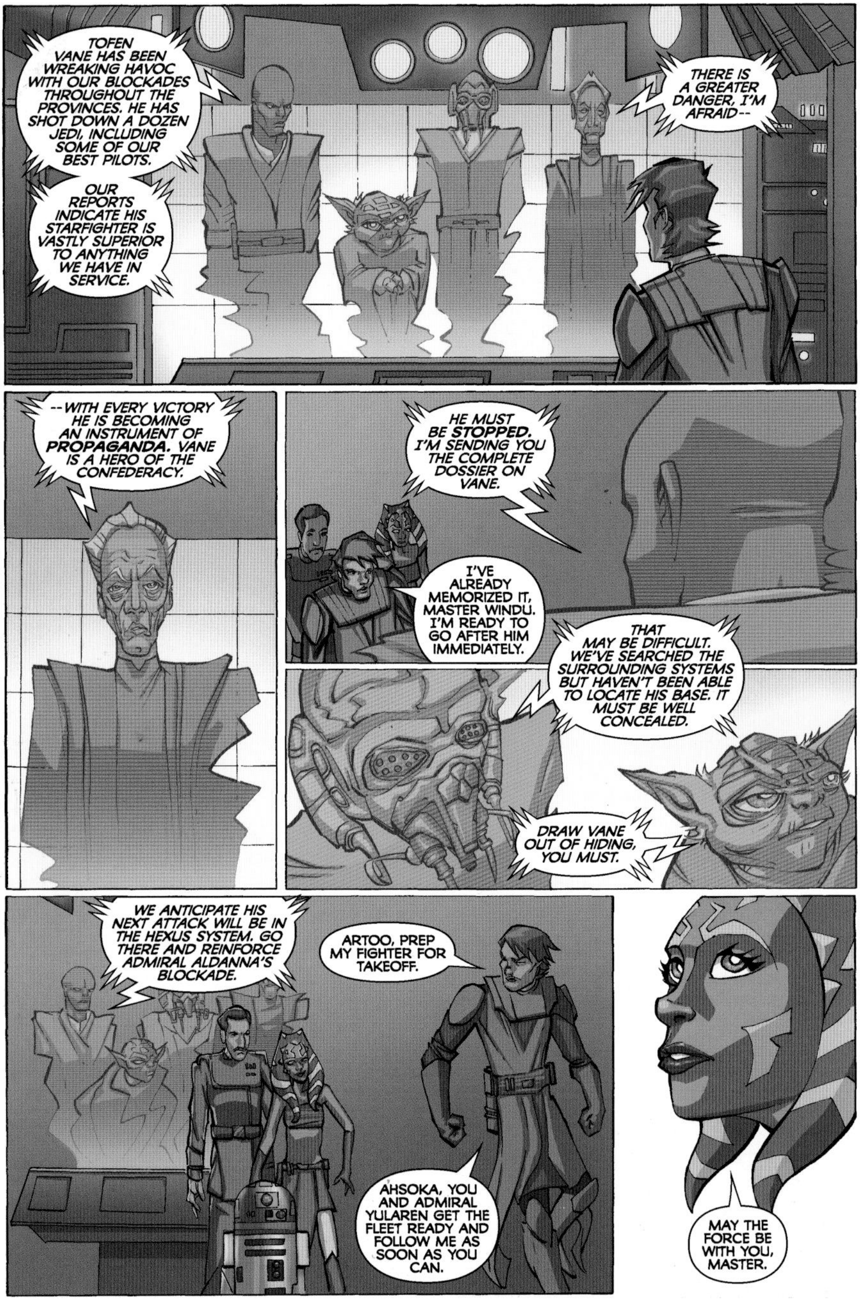
TOFEN VANE HAS BEEN WREAKING HAVOC WITH OUR BLOCKADES THROUGHOUT THE PROVINCES. HE HAS SHOT DOWN A DOZEN JEDI, INCLUDING SOME OF OUR BEST PILOTS.
OUR REPORTS INDICATE HIS STARFIGHTER IS VASTLY SUPERIOR TO ANYTHING WE HAVE IN SERVICE.
THERE IS A GREATER DANGER, I'M AFRAID--
--WITH EVERY VICTORY HE IS BECOMING AN INSTRUMENT OF **PROPAGANDA.** VANE IS A HERO OF THE CONFEDERACY.
HE MUST BE **STOPPED.** I'M SENDING YOU THE COMPLETE DOSSIER ON VANE.
I'VE ALREADY MEMORIZED IT, MASTER WINDU. I'M READY TO GO AFTER HIM IMMEDIATELY.
THAT MAY BE DIFFICULT. WE'VE SEARCHED THE SURROUNDING SYSTEMS BUT HAVEN'T BEEN ABLE TO LOCATE HIS BASE. IT MUST BE WELL CONCEALED.
DRAW VANE OUT OF HIDING, YOU MUST.
WE ANTICIPATE HIS NEXT ATTACK WILL BE IN THE HEXUS SYSTEM. GO THERE AND REINFORCE ADMIRAL ALDANNA'S BLOCKADE.
ARTOO, PREP MY FIGHTER FOR TAKEOFF.
AHSOKA, YOU AND ADMIRAL YULAREN GET THE FLEET READY AND FOLLOW ME AS SOON AS YOU CAN.
MAY THE FORCE BE WITH YOU, MASTER.

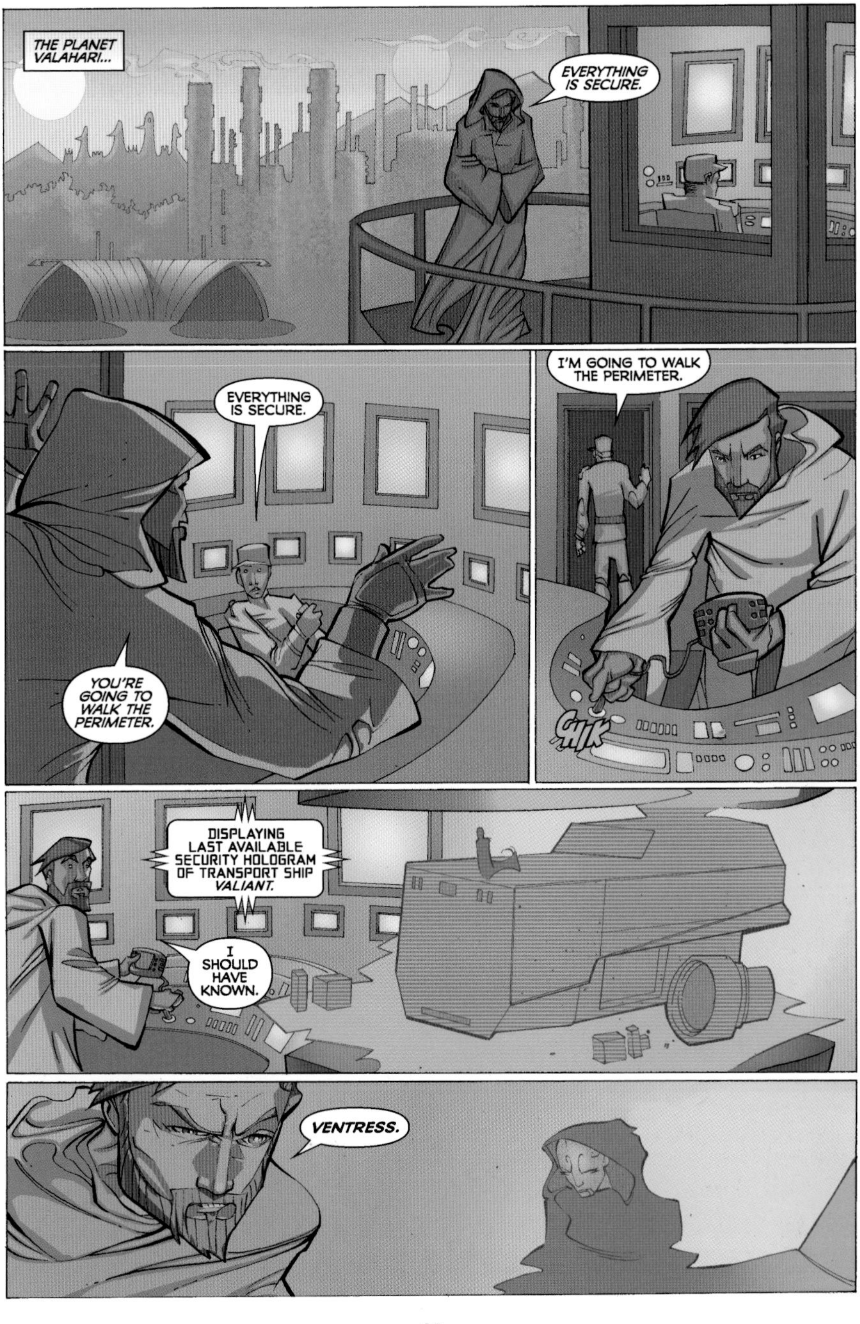
THE PLANET VALAHARI...
EVERYTHING IS SECURE.
EVERYTHING IS SECURE.
YOU'RE GOING TO WALK THE PERIMETER.
I'M GOING TO WALK THE PERIMETER.
CHIK
DISPLAYING LAST AVAILABLE SECURITY HOLOGRAM OF TRANSPORT SHIP VALIANT.
I SHOULD HAVE KNOWN.
VENTRESS.

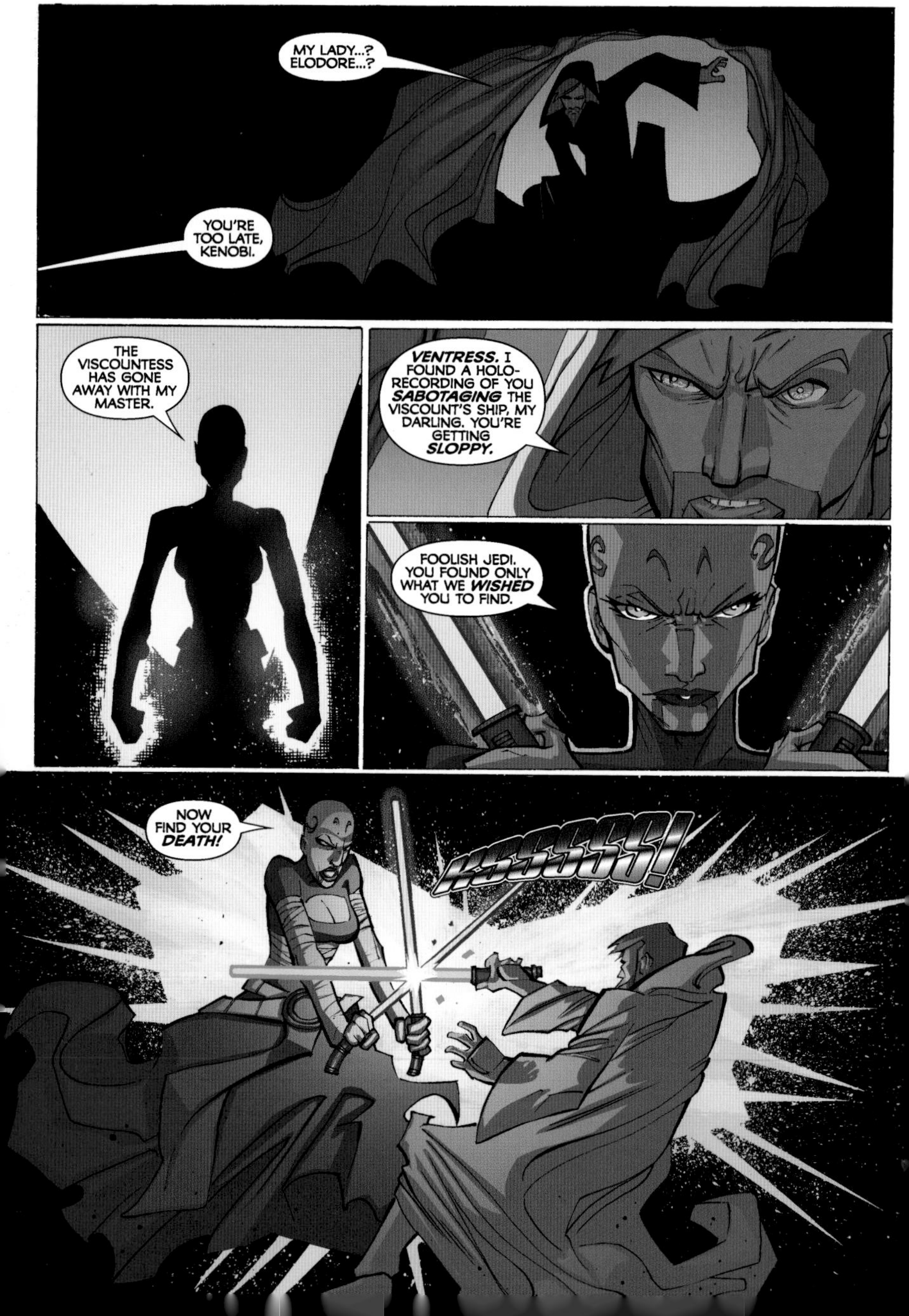
MY LADY...? ELODORE...?
YOU'RE TOO LATE, KENOBI.
THE VISCOUNTESS HAS GONE AWAY WITH MY MASTER.
VENTRESS. I FOUND A HOLO-RECORDING OF YOU SABOTAGING THE VISCOUNT'S SHIP, MY DARLING. YOU'RE GETTING SLOPPY.
FOOLISH JEDI. YOU FOUND ONLY WHAT WE WISHED YOU TO FIND.
NOW FIND YOUR DEATH!
KSSSSSS!

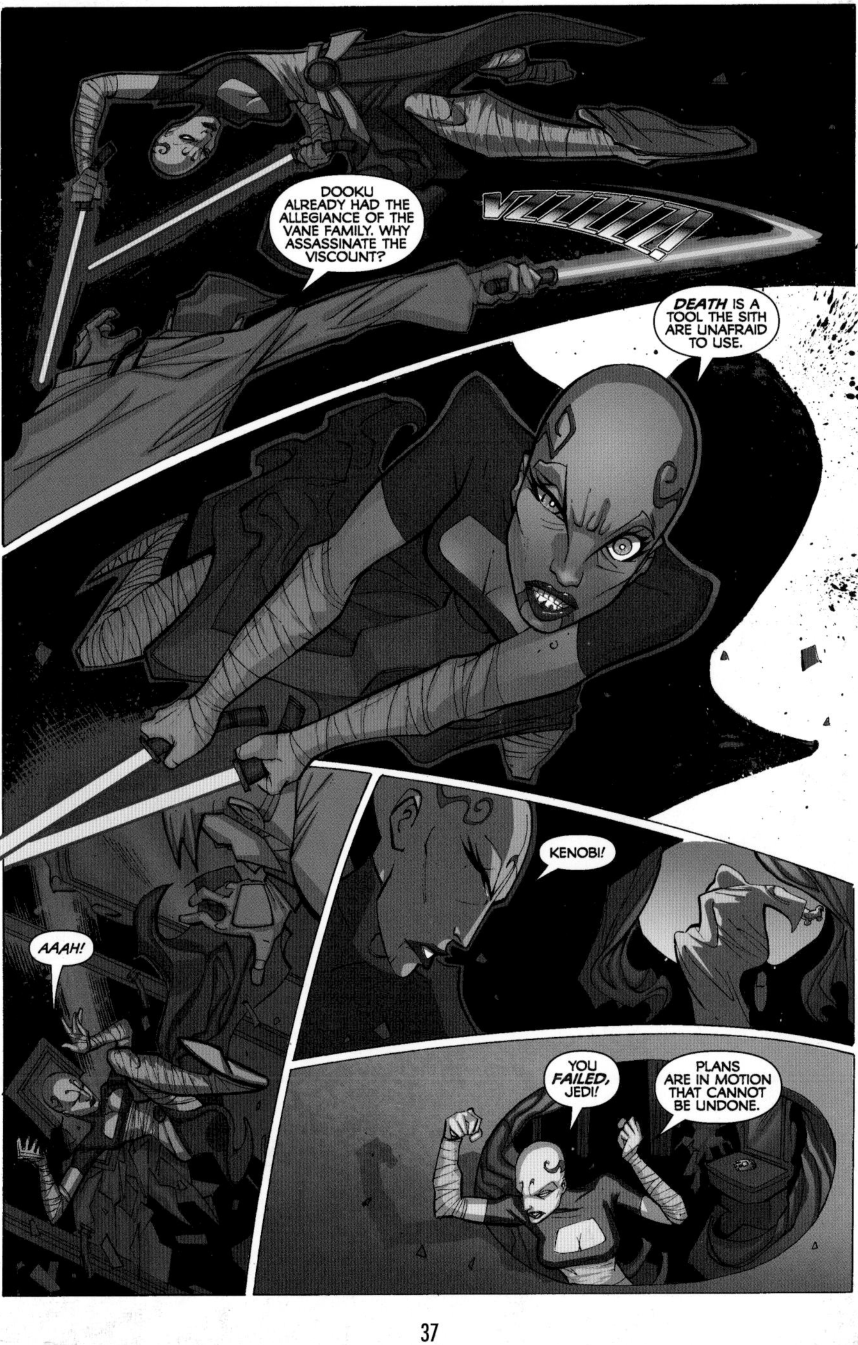
DOOKU ALREADY HAD THE ALLEGIANCE OF THE VANE FAMILY. WHY ASSASSINATE THE VISCOUNT?
VZZZZZT!
DEATH IS A TOOL THE SITH ARE UNAFRAID TO USE.
AAAH!
KENOBI!
YOU FAILED, JEDI!
PLANS ARE IN MOTION THAT CANNOT BE UNDONE.

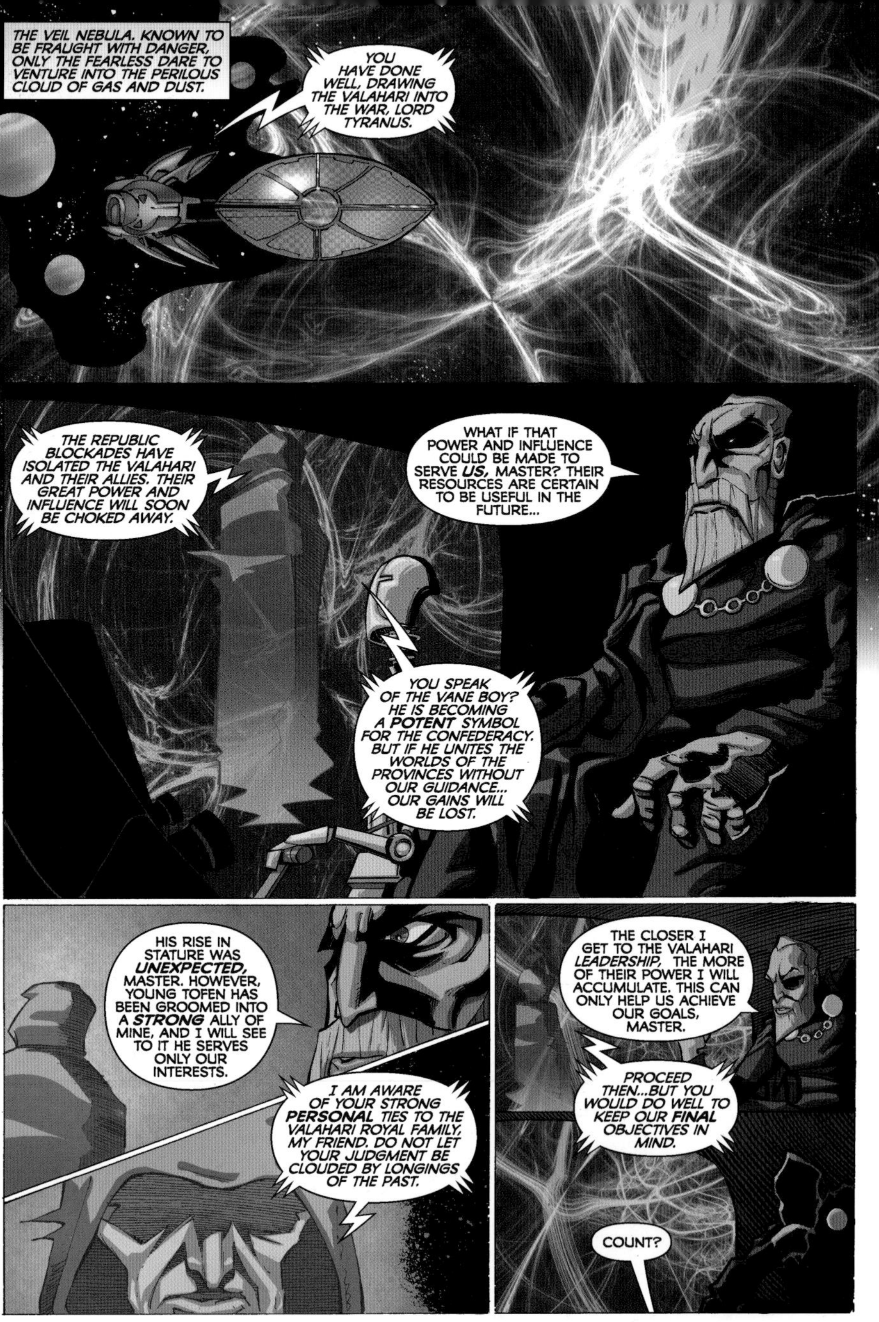
THE VEIL NEBULA. KNOWN TO BE FRAUGHT WITH DANGER, ONLY THE FEARLESS DARE TO VENTURE INTO THE PERILOUS CLOUD OF GAS AND DUST.
YOU HAVE DONE WELL, DRAWING THE VALAHARI INTO THE WAR, LORD TYRANUS.
THE REPUBLIC BLOCKADES HAVE ISOLATED THE VALAHARI AND THEIR ALLIES. THEIR GREAT POWER AND INFLUENCE WILL SOON BE CHOKED AWAY.
WHAT IF THAT POWER AND INFLUENCE COULD BE MADE TO SERVE US, MASTER? THEIR RESOURCES ARE CERTAIN TO BE USEFUL IN THE FUTURE...
YOU SPEAK OF THE VANE BOY? HE IS BECOMING A POTENT SYMBOL FOR THE CONFEDERACY. BUT IF HE UNITES THE WORLDS OF THE PROVINCES WITHOUT OUR GUIDANCE... OUR GAINS WILL BE LOST.
HIS RISE IN STATURE WAS UNEXPECTED, MASTER. HOWEVER, YOUNG TOFEN HAS BEEN GROOMED INTO A STRONG ALLY OF MINE, AND I WILL SEE TO IT HE SERVES ONLY OUR INTERESTS.
I AM AWARE OF YOUR STRONG PERSONAL TIES TO THE VALAHARI ROYAL FAMILY, MY FRIEND. DO NOT LET YOUR JUDGMENT BE CLOUDED BY LONGINGS OF THE PAST.
THE CLOSER I GET TO THE VALAHARI LEADERSHIP, THE MORE OF THEIR POWER I WILL ACCUMULATE. THIS CAN ONLY HELP US ACHIEVE OUR GOALS, MASTER.
PROCEED THEN...BUT YOU WOULD DO WELL TO KEEP OUR FINAL OBJECTIVES IN MIND.
COUNT?

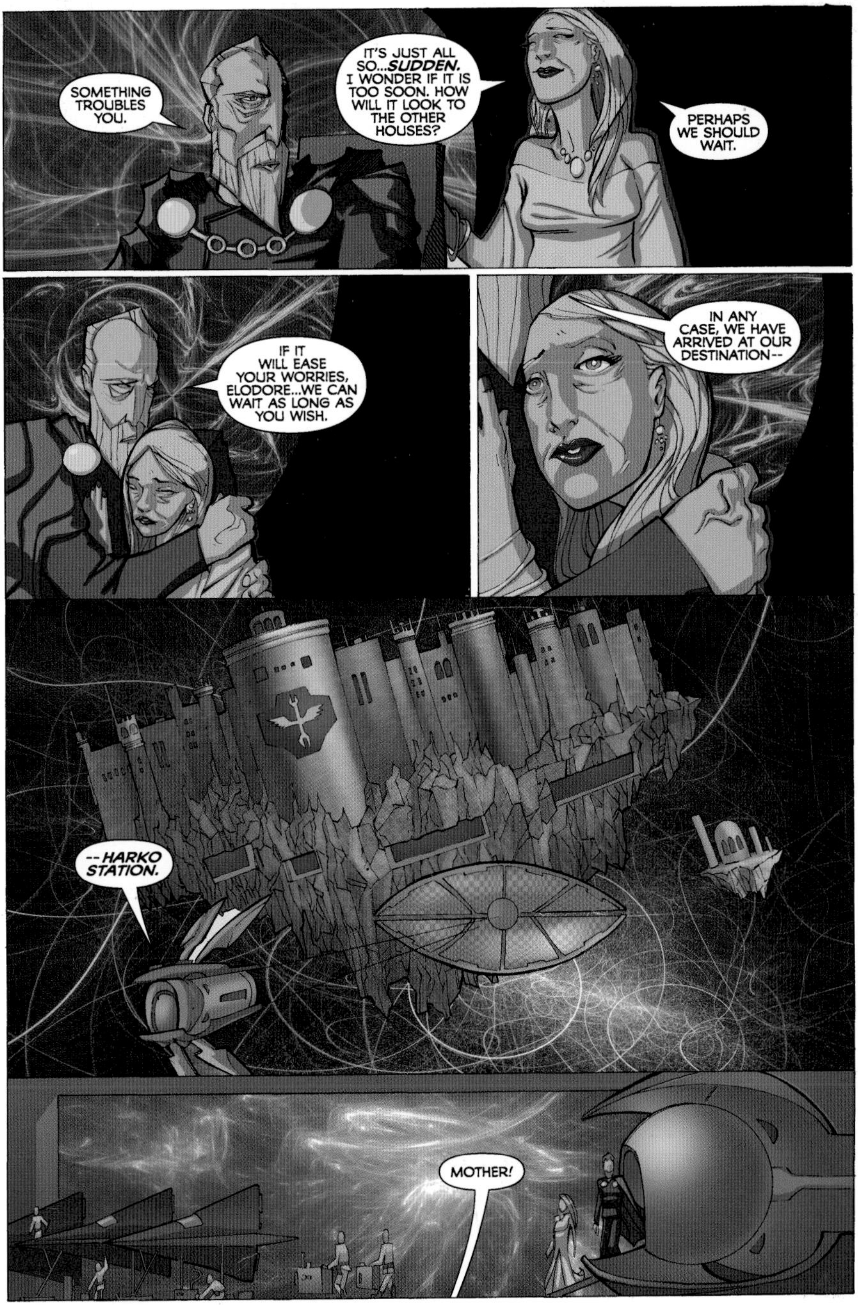
SOMETHING TROUBLES YOU.
IT'S JUST ALL SO...***SUDDEN.*** I WONDER IF IT IS TOO SOON. HOW WILL IT LOOK TO THE OTHER HOUSES?
PERHAPS WE SHOULD WAIT.
IF IT WILL EASE YOUR WORRIES, ELODORE...WE CAN WAIT AS LONG AS YOU WISH.
IN ANY CASE, WE HAVE ARRIVED AT OUR DESTINATION--
--***HARKO STATION.***
MOTHER!

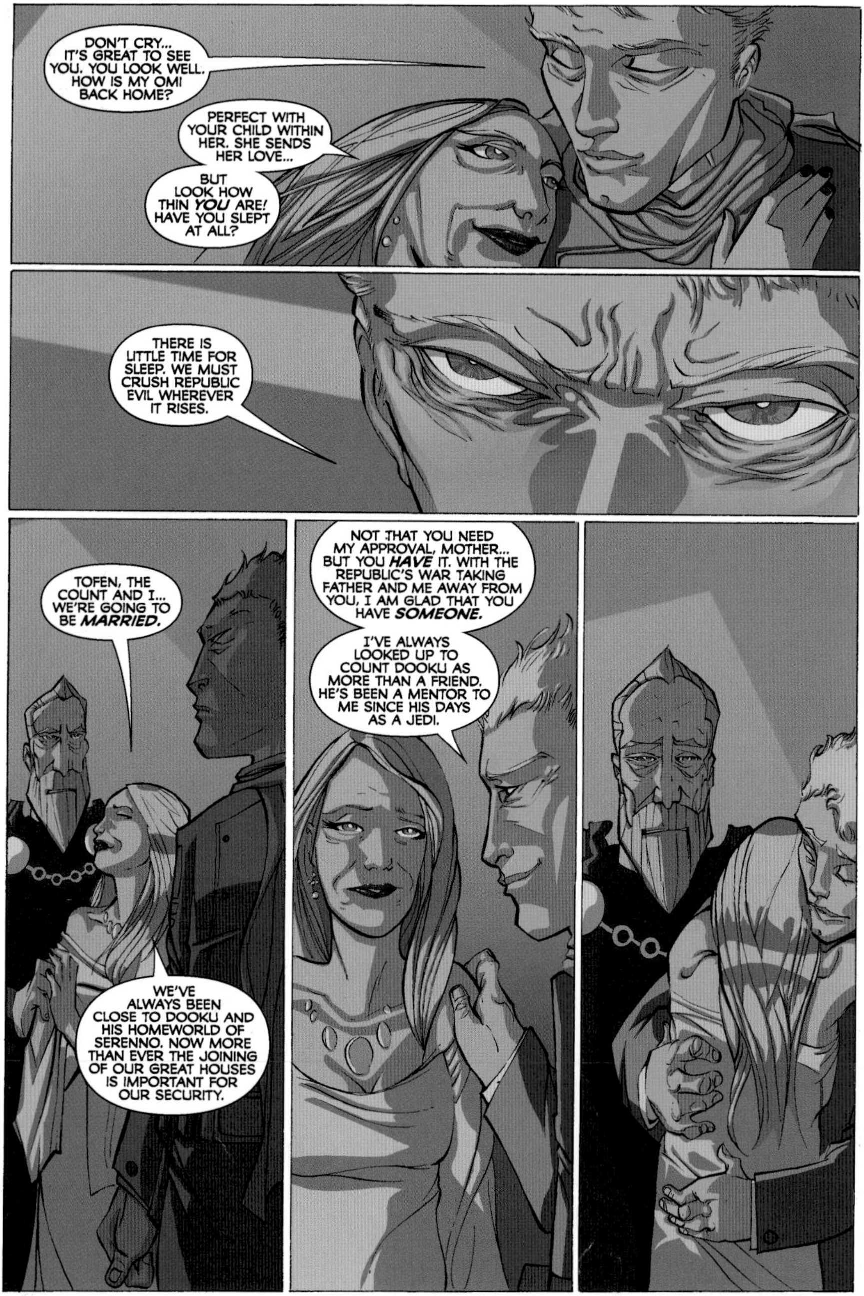

DON'T CRY... IT'S GREAT TO SEE YOU. YOU LOOK WELL. HOW IS MY OMI BACK HOME?
PERFECT WITH YOUR CHILD WITHIN HER. SHE SENDS HER LOVE...
BUT LOOK HOW THIN *YOU* ARE! HAVE YOU SLEPT AT ALL?
THERE IS LITTLE TIME FOR SLEEP. WE MUST CRUSH REPUBLIC EVIL WHEREVER IT RISES.
TOFEN, THE COUNT AND I... WE'RE GOING TO BE ***MARRIED.***
WE'VE ALWAYS BEEN CLOSE TO DOOKU AND HIS HOMEWORLD OF SERENNO. NOW MORE THAN EVER THE JOINING OF OUR GREAT HOUSES IS IMPORTANT FOR OUR SECURITY.
NOT THAT YOU NEED MY APPROVAL, MOTHER... BUT YOU ***HAVE*** IT. WITH THE REPUBLIC'S WAR TAKING FATHER AND ME AWAY FROM YOU, I AM GLAD THAT YOU HAVE ***SOMEONE.***
I'VE ALWAYS LOOKED UP TO COUNT DOOKU AS MORE THAN A FRIEND. HE'S BEEN A MENTOR TO ME SINCE HIS DAYS AS A JEDI.

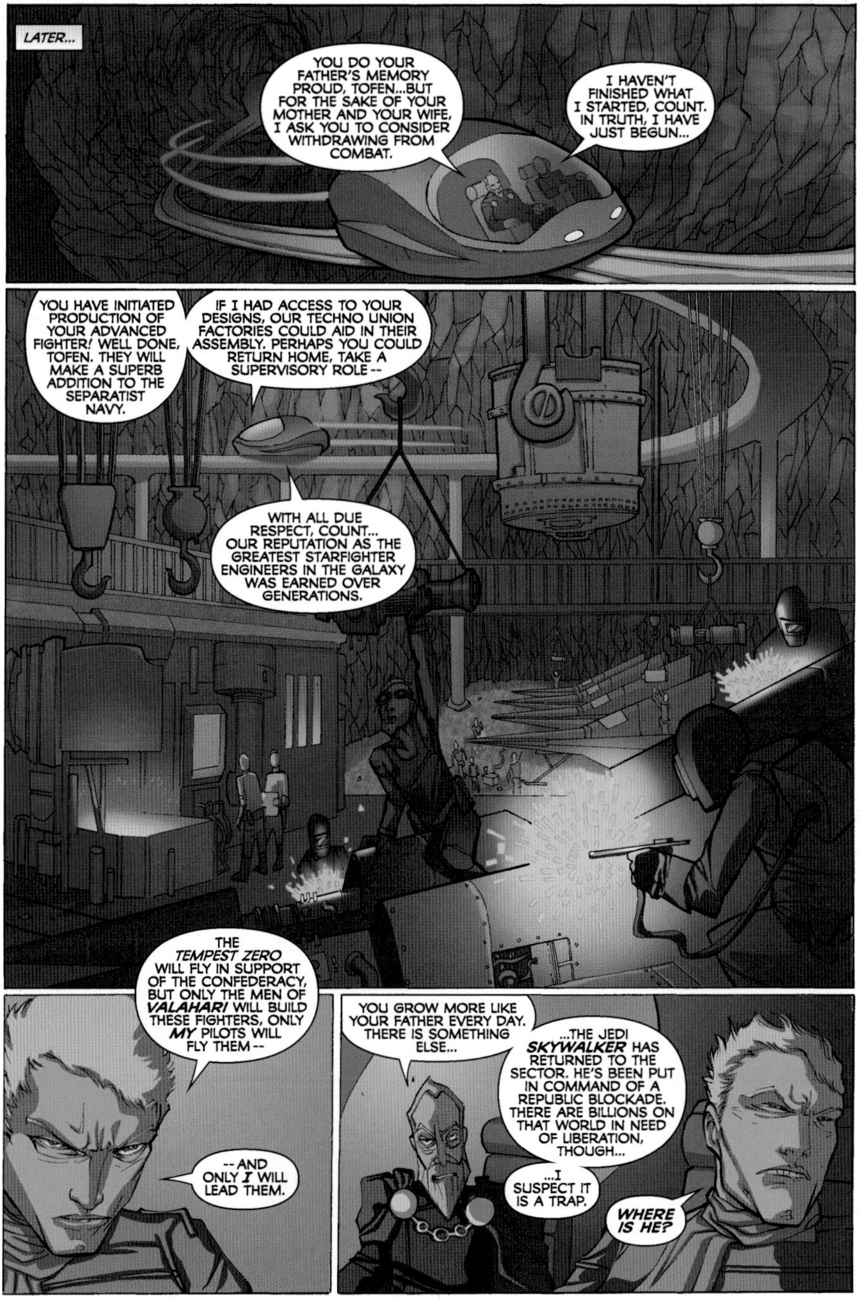
LATER...
YOU DO YOUR FATHER'S MEMORY PROUD, TOFEN...BUT FOR THE SAKE OF YOUR MOTHER AND YOUR WIFE, I ASK YOU TO CONSIDER WITHDRAWING FROM COMBAT.
I HAVEN'T FINISHED WHAT I STARTED, COUNT. IN TRUTH, I HAVE JUST BEGUN...
YOU HAVE INITIATED PRODUCTION OF YOUR ADVANCED FIGHTER! WELL DONE, TOFEN. THEY WILL MAKE A SUPERB ADDITION TO THE SEPARATIST NAVY.
IF I HAD ACCESS TO YOUR DESIGNS, OUR TECHNO UNION FACTORIES COULD AID IN THEIR ASSEMBLY. PERHAPS YOU COULD RETURN HOME, TAKE A SUPERVISORY ROLE --
WITH ALL DUE RESPECT, COUNT... OUR REPUTATION AS THE GREATEST STARFIGHTER ENGINEERS IN THE GALAXY WAS EARNED OVER GENERATIONS.
THE *TEMPEST ZERO* WILL FLY IN SUPPORT OF THE CONFEDERACY, BUT ONLY THE MEN OF ***VALAHARI*** WILL BUILD THESE FIGHTERS, ONLY ***MY*** PILOTS WILL FLY THEM --
-- AND ONLY ***I*** WILL LEAD THEM.
YOU GROW MORE LIKE YOUR FATHER EVERY DAY. THERE IS SOMETHING ELSE...
...THE JEDI ***SKYWALKER*** HAS RETURNED TO THE SECTOR. HE'S BEEN PUT IN COMMAND OF A REPUBLIC BLOCKADE. THERE ARE BILLIONS ON THAT WORLD IN NEED OF LIBERATION, THOUGH...
...I SUSPECT IT IS A TRAP.
WHERE IS HE?

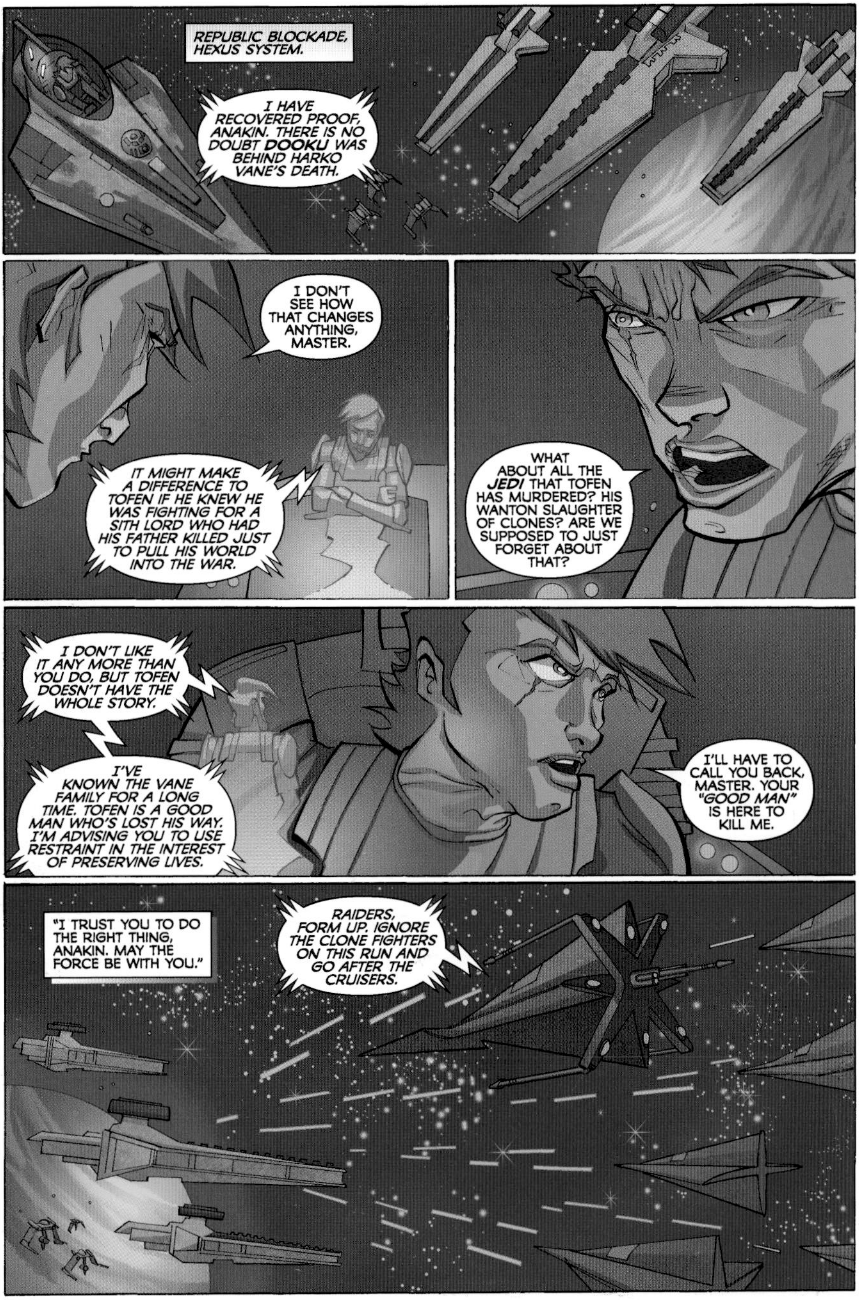
REPUBLIC BLOCKADE, HEXUS SYSTEM.
I HAVE RECOVERED PROOF, ANAKIN. THERE IS NO DOUBT DOOKU WAS BEHIND HARKO VANE'S DEATH.
I DON'T SEE HOW THAT CHANGES ANYTHING, MASTER.
IT MIGHT MAKE A DIFFERENCE TO TOFEN IF HE KNEW HE WAS FIGHTING FOR A SITH LORD WHO HAD HIS FATHER KILLED JUST TO PULL HIS WORLD INTO THE WAR.
WHAT ABOUT ALL THE JEDI THAT TOFEN HAS MURDERED? HIS WANTON SLAUGHTER OF CLONES? ARE WE SUPPOSED TO JUST FORGET ABOUT THAT?
I DON'T LIKE IT ANY MORE THAN YOU DO, BUT TOFEN DOESN'T HAVE THE WHOLE STORY.
I'VE KNOWN THE VANE FAMILY FOR A LONG TIME. TOFEN IS A GOOD MAN WHO'S LOST HIS WAY. I'M ADVISING YOU TO USE RESTRAINT IN THE INTEREST OF PRESERVING LIVES.
I'LL HAVE TO CALL YOU BACK, MASTER. YOUR "GOOD MAN" IS HERE TO KILL ME.
"I TRUST YOU TO DO THE RIGHT THING, ANAKIN. MAY THE FORCE BE WITH YOU."
RAIDERS, FORM UP. IGNORE THE CLONE FIGHTERS ON THIS RUN AND GO AFTER THE CRUISERS.

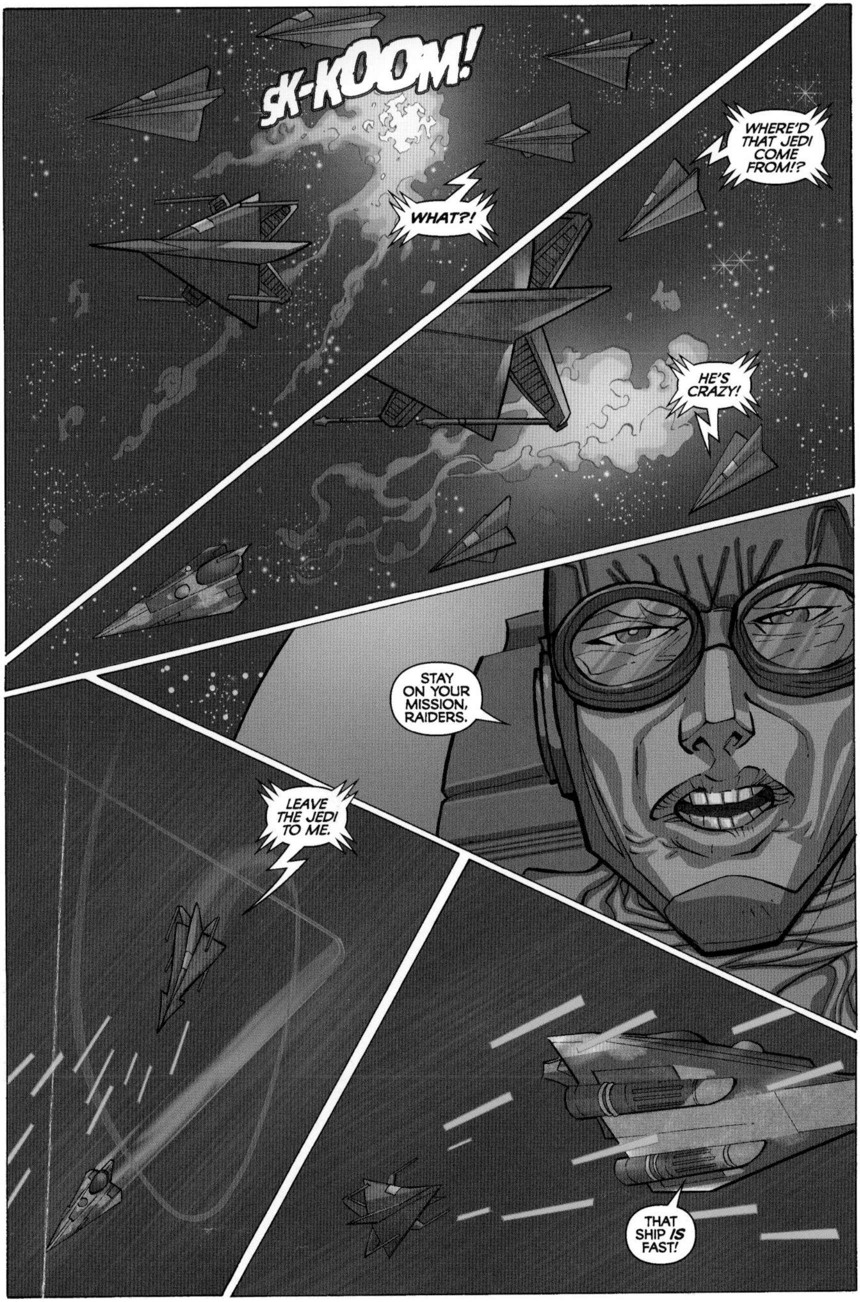
SK-KOOM!
WHAT?!
WHERE'D THAT JEDI COME FROM!?
HE'S CRAZY!
STAY ON YOUR MISSION, RAIDERS.
LEAVE THE JEDI TO ME.
THAT SHIP *IS* FAST!

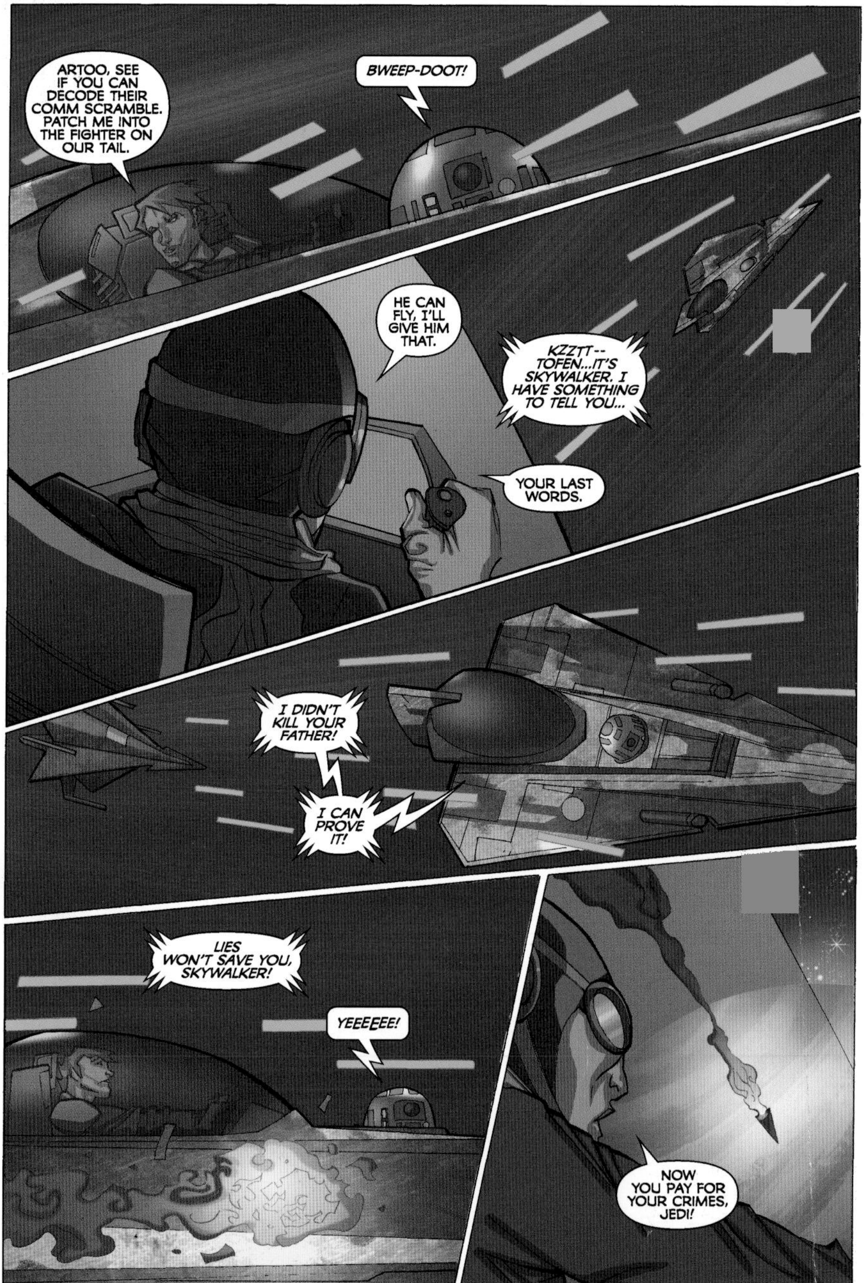
ARTOO, SEE IF YOU CAN DECODE THEIR COMM SCRAMBLE. PATCH ME INTO THE FIGHTER ON OUR TAIL.
BWEEP-DOOT!
HE CAN FLY, I'LL GIVE HIM THAT.
KZZTT-- TOFEN...IT'S SKYWALKER. I HAVE SOMETHING TO TELL YOU...
YOUR LAST WORDS.
I DIDN'T KILL YOUR FATHER!
I CAN PROVE IT!
LIES WON'T SAVE YOU, SKYWALKER!
YEEEEEE!
NOW YOU PAY FOR YOUR CRIMES, JEDI!

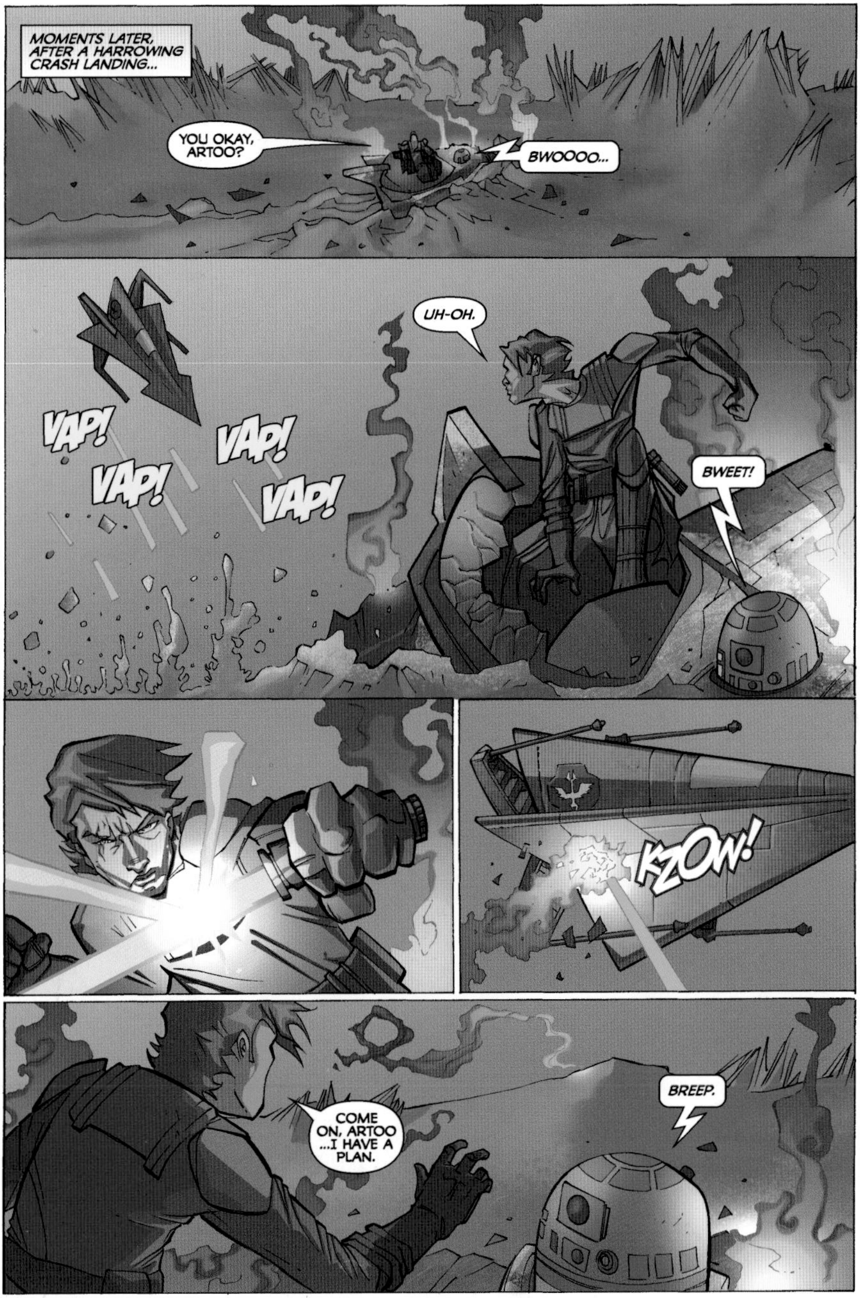
MOMENTS LATER, AFTER A HARROWING CRASH LANDING...
YOU OKAY, ARTOO?
BWOOOO...
UH-OH.
VAP!
VAP!
VAP!
VAP!
BWEET!
KZOW!
COME ON, ARTOO ...I HAVE A PLAN.
BREEP.

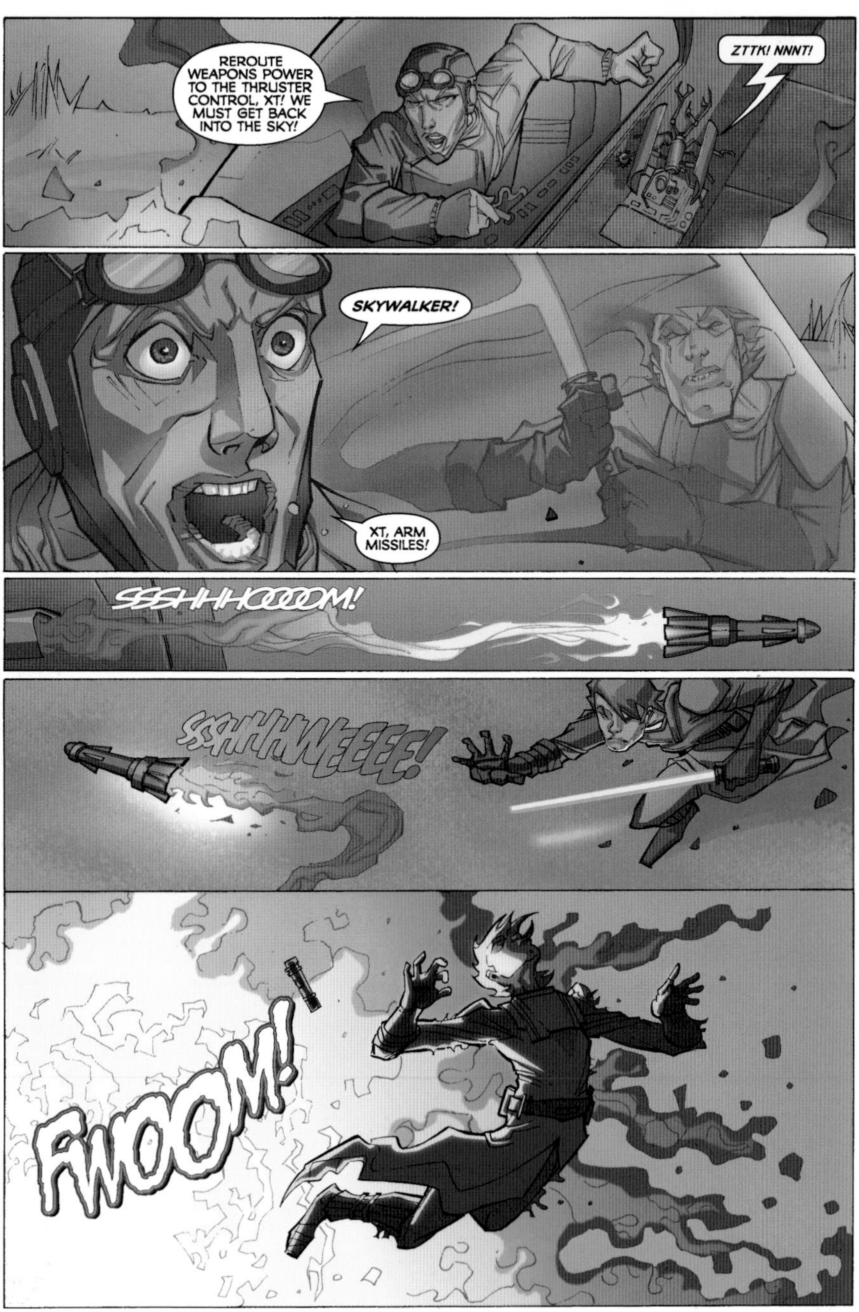
REROUTE WEAPONS POWER TO THE THRUSTER CONTROL, XT! WE MUST GET BACK INTO THE SKY!
ZTTK! NNNT!
SKYWALKER!
XT, ARM MISSILES!
SSSHHHOOOOM!
SSSHHHWEEEE!
FWOOM!

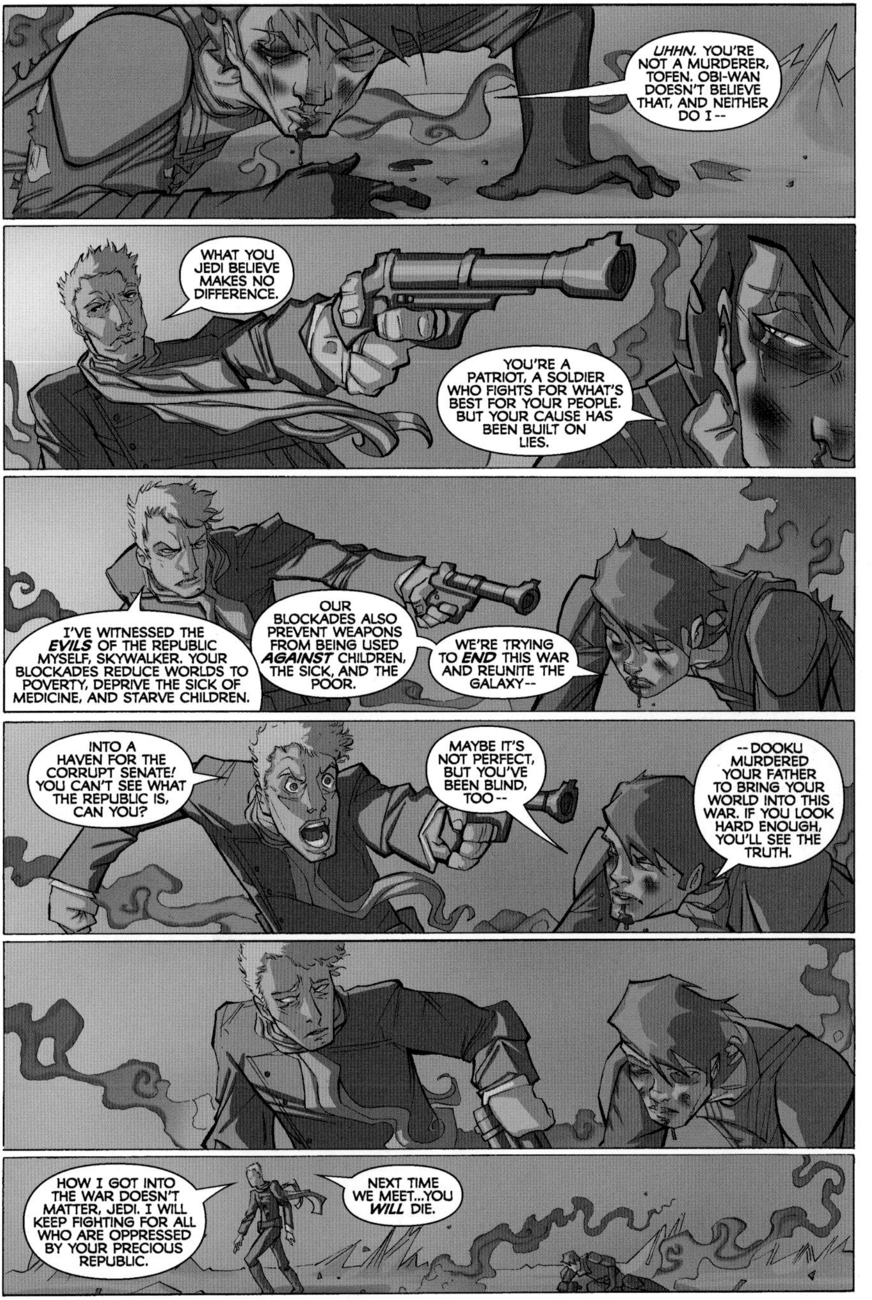
UHHN. YOU'RE NOT A MURDERER, TOFEN. OBI-WAN DOESN'T BELIEVE THAT, AND NEITHER DO I--
WHAT YOU JEDI BELIEVE MAKES NO DIFFERENCE.
YOU'RE A PATRIOT, A SOLDIER WHO FIGHTS FOR WHAT'S BEST FOR YOUR PEOPLE. BUT YOUR CAUSE HAS BEEN BUILT ON LIES.
I'VE WITNESSED THE EVILS OF THE REPUBLIC MYSELF, SKYWALKER. YOUR BLOCKADES REDUCE WORLDS TO POVERTY, DEPRIVE THE SICK OF MEDICINE, AND STARVE CHILDREN.
OUR BLOCKADES ALSO PREVENT WEAPONS FROM BEING USED AGAINST CHILDREN, THE SICK, AND THE POOR.
WE'RE TRYING TO END THIS WAR AND REUNITE THE GALAXY--
INTO A HAVEN FOR THE CORRUPT SENATE! YOU CAN'T SEE WHAT THE REPUBLIC IS, CAN YOU?
MAYBE IT'S NOT PERFECT, BUT YOU'VE BEEN BLIND, TOO--
--DOOKU MURDERED YOUR FATHER TO BRING YOUR WORLD INTO THIS WAR. IF YOU LOOK HARD ENOUGH, YOU'LL SEE THE TRUTH.
HOW I GOT INTO THE WAR DOESN'T MATTER, JEDI. I WILL KEEP FIGHTING FOR ALL WHO ARE OPPRESSED BY YOUR PRECIOUS REPUBLIC.
NEXT TIME WE MEET...YOU WILL DIE.

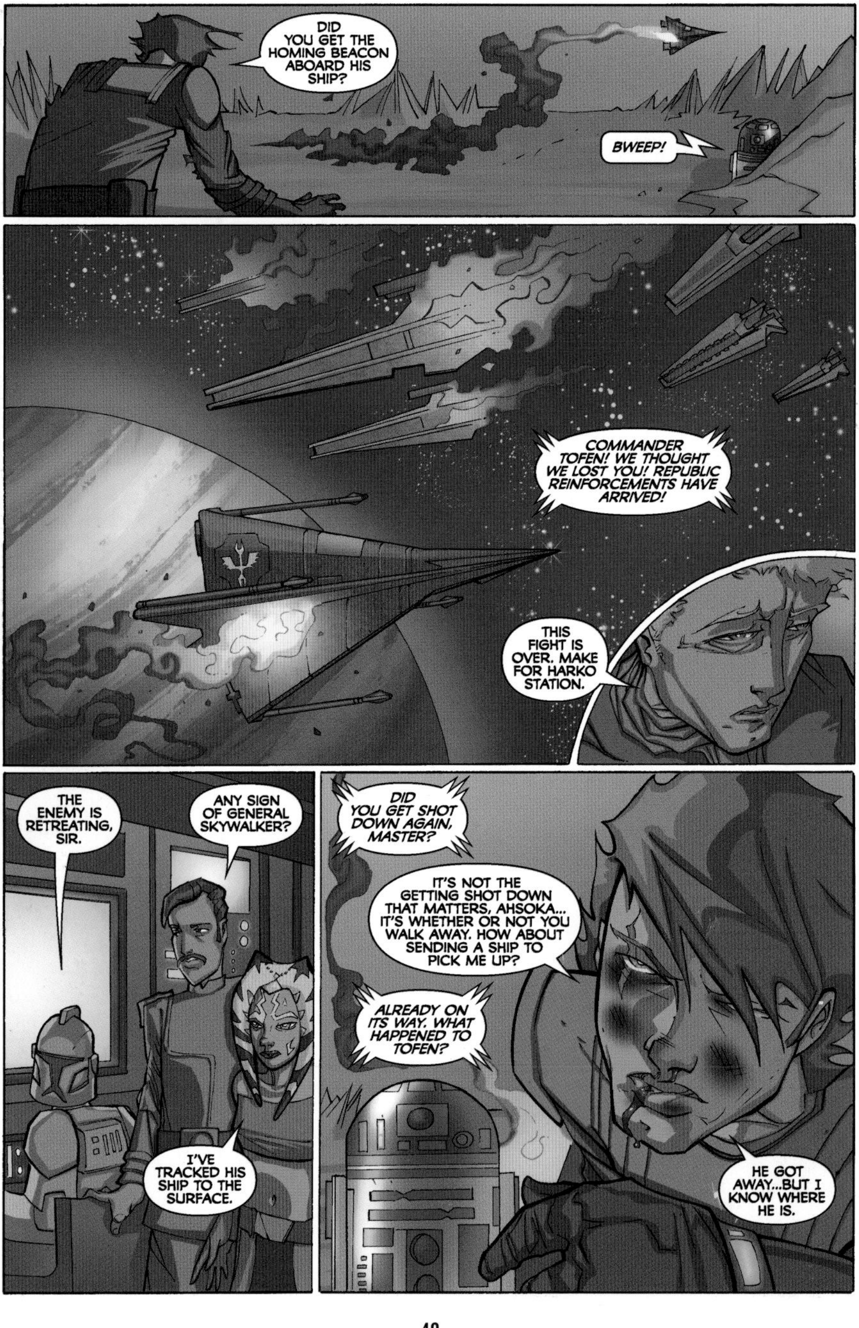
DID YOU GET THE HOMING BEACON ABOARD HIS SHIP?
BWEEP!
COMMANDER TOFEN! WE THOUGHT WE LOST YOU! REPUBLIC REINFORCEMENTS HAVE ARRIVED!
THIS FIGHT IS OVER. MAKE FOR HARKO STATION.
THE ENEMY IS RETREATING, SIR.
ANY SIGN OF GENERAL SKYWALKER?
I'VE TRACKED HIS SHIP TO THE SURFACE.
DID YOU GET SHOT DOWN AGAIN, MASTER?
IT'S NOT THE GETTING SHOT DOWN THAT MATTERS, AHSOKA... IT'S WHETHER OR NOT YOU WALK AWAY. HOW ABOUT SENDING A SHIP TO PICK ME UP?
ALREADY ON ITS WAY. WHAT HAPPENED TO TOFEN?
HE GOT AWAY...BUT I KNOW WHERE HE IS.

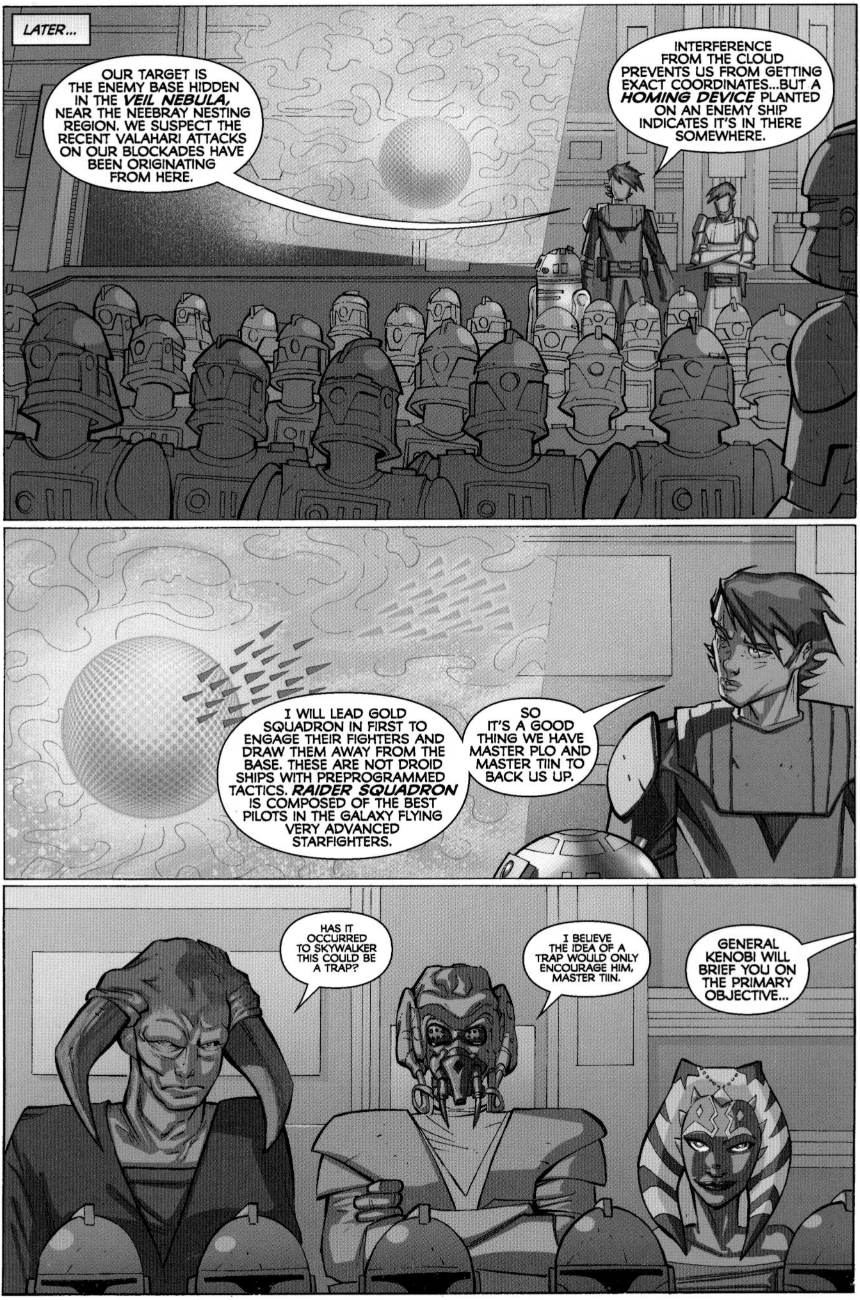
LATER...
OUR TARGET IS THE ENEMY BASE HIDDEN IN THE VEIL NEBULA, NEAR THE NEEBRAY NESTING REGION. WE SUSPECT THE RECENT VALAHARI ATTACKS ON OUR BLOCKADES HAVE BEEN ORIGINATING FROM HERE.
INTERFERENCE FROM THE CLOUD PREVENTS US FROM GETTING EXACT COORDINATES...BUT A HOMING DEVICE PLANTED ON AN ENEMY SHIP INDICATES IT'S IN THERE SOMEWHERE.
I WILL LEAD GOLD SQUADRON IN FIRST TO ENGAGE THEIR FIGHTERS AND DRAW THEM AWAY FROM THE BASE. THESE ARE NOT DROID SHIPS WITH PREPROGRAMMED TACTICS. RAIDER SQUADRON IS COMPOSED OF THE BEST PILOTS IN THE GALAXY FLYING VERY ADVANCED STARFIGHTERS.
SO IT'S A GOOD THING WE HAVE MASTER PLO AND MASTER TIIN TO BACK US UP.
HAS IT OCCURRED TO SKYWALKER THIS COULD BE A TRAP?
I BELIEVE THE IDEA OF A TRAP WOULD ONLY ENCOURAGE HIM, MASTER TIIN.
GENERAL KENOBI WILL BRIEF YOU ON THE PRIMARY OBJECTIVE...

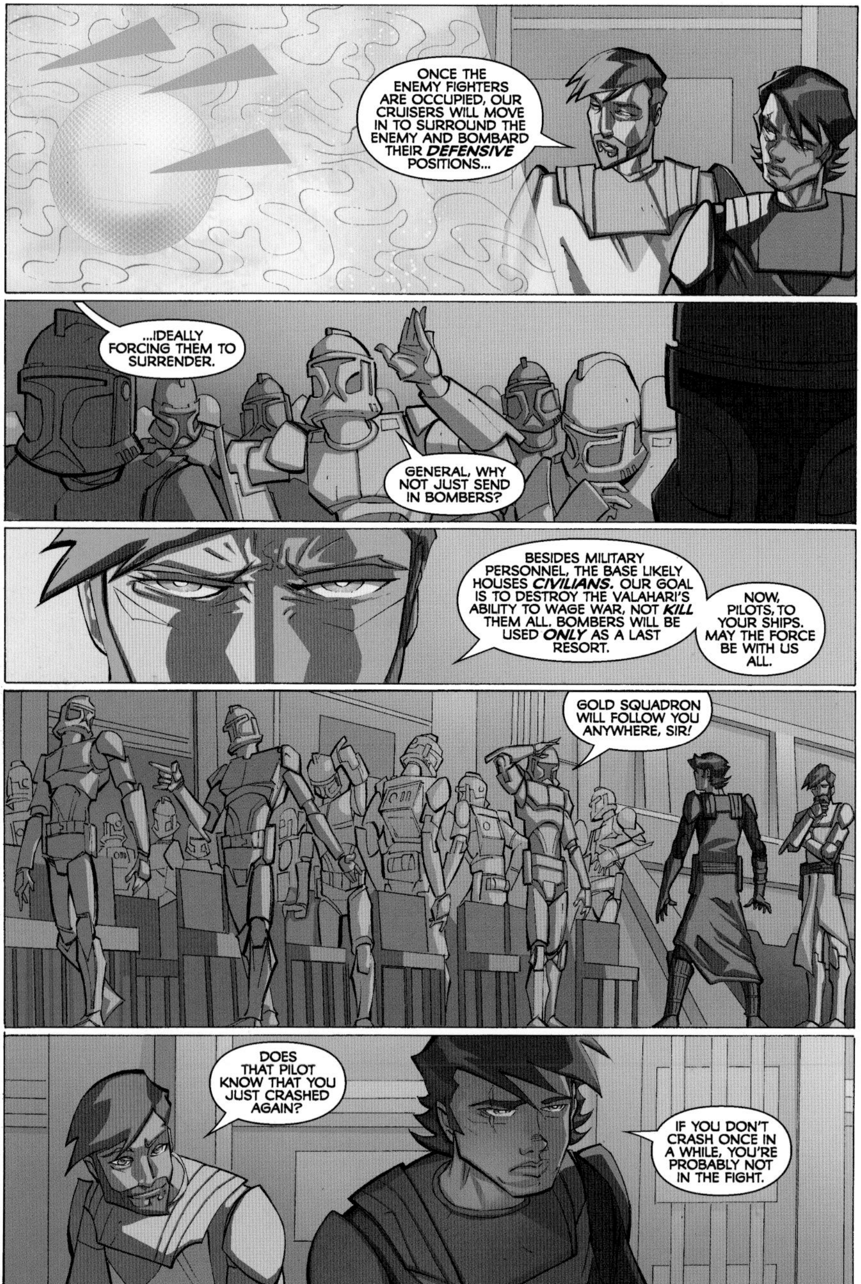
ONCE THE ENEMY FIGHTERS ARE OCCUPIED, OUR CRUISERS WILL MOVE IN TO SURROUND THE ENEMY AND BOMBARD THEIR *DEFENSIVE* POSITIONS...
...IDEALLY FORCING THEM TO SURRENDER.
GENERAL, WHY NOT JUST SEND IN BOMBERS?
BESIDES MILITARY PERSONNEL, THE BASE LIKELY HOUSES *CIVILIANS.* OUR GOAL IS TO DESTROY THE VALAHARI'S ABILITY TO WAGE WAR, NOT *KILL* THEM ALL. BOMBERS WILL BE USED *ONLY* AS A LAST RESORT.
NOW, PILOTS, TO YOUR SHIPS. MAY THE FORCE BE WITH US ALL.
GOLD SQUADRON WILL FOLLOW YOU ANYWHERE, SIR!
DOES THAT PILOT KNOW THAT YOU JUST CRASHED AGAIN?
IF YOU DON'T CRASH ONCE IN A WHILE, YOU'RE PROBABLY NOT IN THE FIGHT.

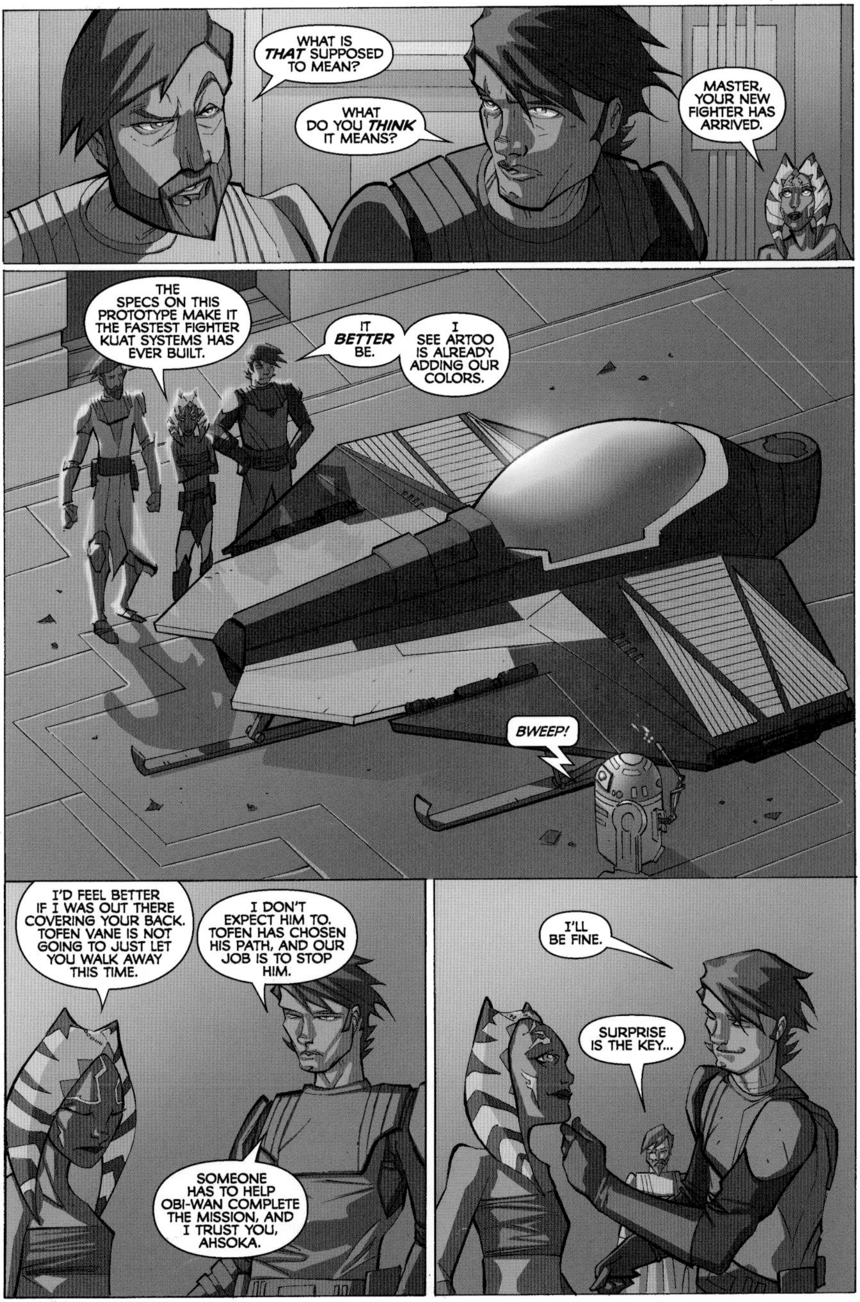
WHAT IS *THAT* SUPPOSED TO MEAN?
WHAT DO YOU *THINK* IT MEANS?
MASTER, YOUR NEW FIGHTER HAS ARRIVED.
THE SPECS ON THIS PROTOTYPE MAKE IT THE FASTEST FIGHTER KUAT SYSTEMS HAS EVER BUILT.
IT *BETTER* BE.
I SEE ARTOO IS ALREADY ADDING OUR COLORS.
BWEEP!
I'D FEEL BETTER IF I WAS OUT THERE COVERING YOUR BACK. TOFEN VANE IS NOT GOING TO JUST LET YOU WALK AWAY THIS TIME.
I DON'T EXPECT HIM TO. TOFEN HAS CHOSEN HIS PATH, AND OUR JOB IS TO STOP HIM.
SOMEONE HAS TO HELP OBI-WAN COMPLETE THE MISSION, AND I TRUST YOU, AHSOKA.
I'LL BE FINE.
SURPRISE IS THE KEY...

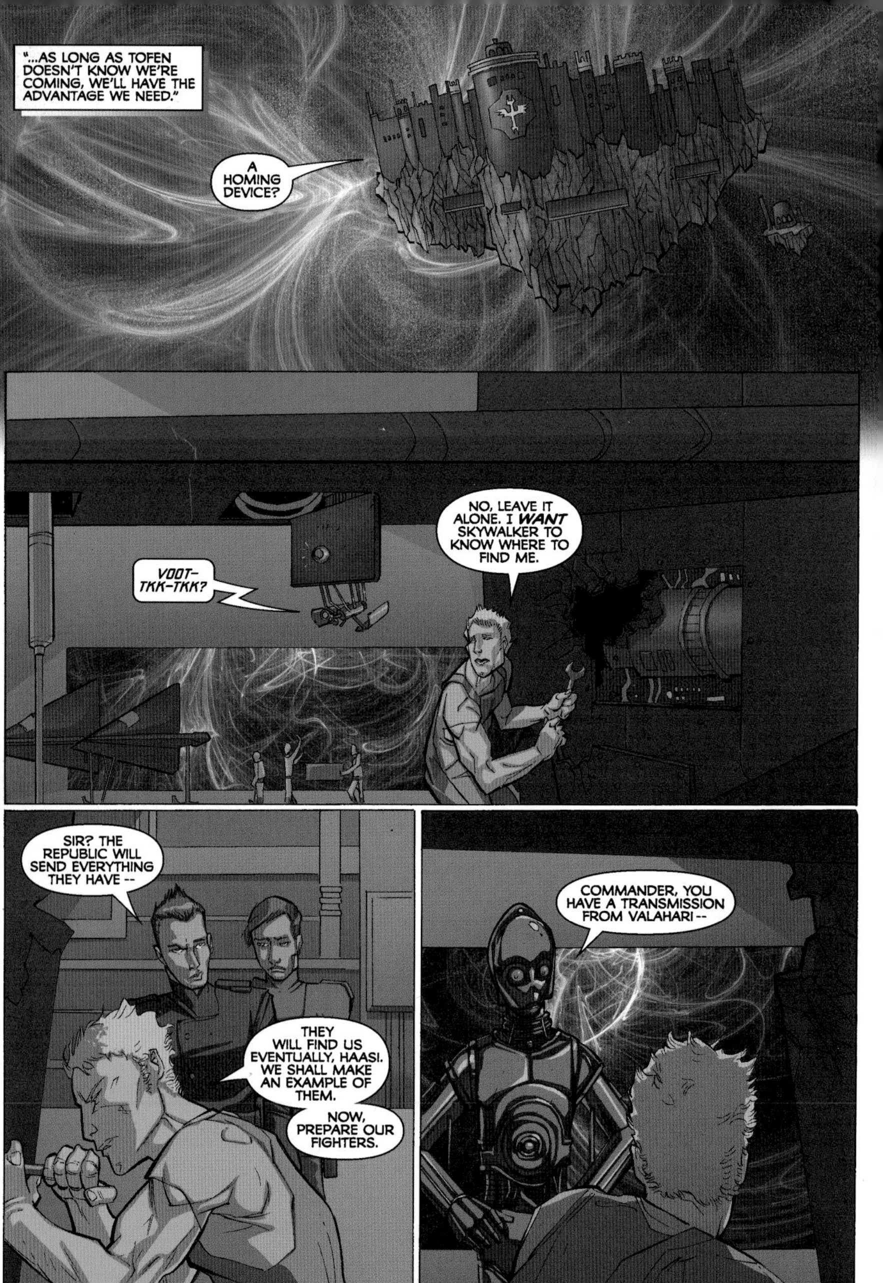
"...AS LONG AS TOFEN DOESN'T KNOW WE'RE COMING, WE'LL HAVE THE ADVANTAGE WE NEED."
A HOMING DEVICE?
VOOT-TKK-TKK?
NO, LEAVE IT ALONE. I *WANT* SKYWALKER TO KNOW WHERE TO FIND ME.
SIR? THE REPUBLIC WILL SEND EVERYTHING THEY HAVE --
THEY WILL FIND US EVENTUALLY, HAASI. WE SHALL MAKE AN EXAMPLE OF THEM.
NOW, PREPARE OUR FIGHTERS.
COMMANDER, YOU HAVE A TRANSMISSION FROM VALAHARI --

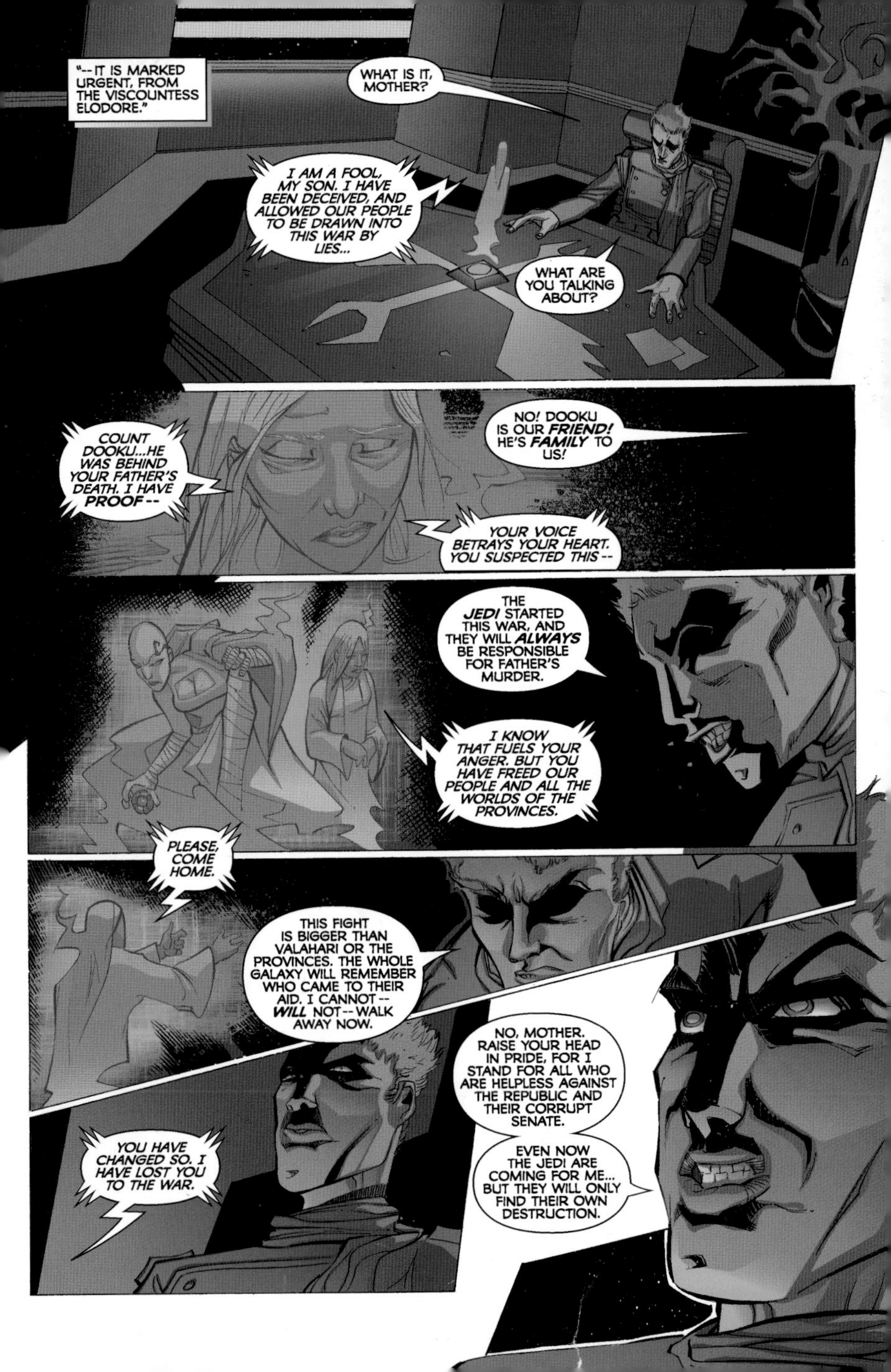
"--IT IS MARKED URGENT, FROM THE VISCOUNTESS ELODORE."
WHAT IS IT, MOTHER?
I AM A FOOL, MY SON. I HAVE BEEN DECEIVED, AND ALLOWED OUR PEOPLE TO BE DRAWN INTO THIS WAR BY LIES...
WHAT ARE YOU TALKING ABOUT?
COUNT DOOKU...HE WAS BEHIND YOUR FATHER'S DEATH. I HAVE PROOF--
NO! DOOKU IS OUR FRIEND! HE'S FAMILY TO US!
YOUR VOICE BETRAYS YOUR HEART. YOU SUSPECTED THIS--
THE JEDI STARTED THIS WAR, AND THEY WILL ALWAYS BE RESPONSIBLE FOR FATHER'S MURDER.
I KNOW THAT FUELS YOUR ANGER. BUT YOU HAVE FREED OUR PEOPLE AND ALL THE WORLDS OF THE PROVINCES.
PLEASE, COME HOME.
THIS FIGHT IS BIGGER THAN VALAHARI OR THE PROVINCES. THE WHOLE GALAXY WILL REMEMBER WHO CAME TO THEIR AID. I CANNOT--WILL NOT--WALK AWAY NOW.
YOU HAVE CHANGED SO. I HAVE LOST YOU TO THE WAR.
NO, MOTHER. RAISE YOUR HEAD IN PRIDE, FOR I STAND FOR ALL WHO ARE HELPLESS AGAINST THE REPUBLIC AND THEIR CORRUPT SENATE.
EVEN NOW THE JEDI ARE COMING FOR ME... BUT THEY WILL ONLY FIND THEIR OWN DESTRUCTION.

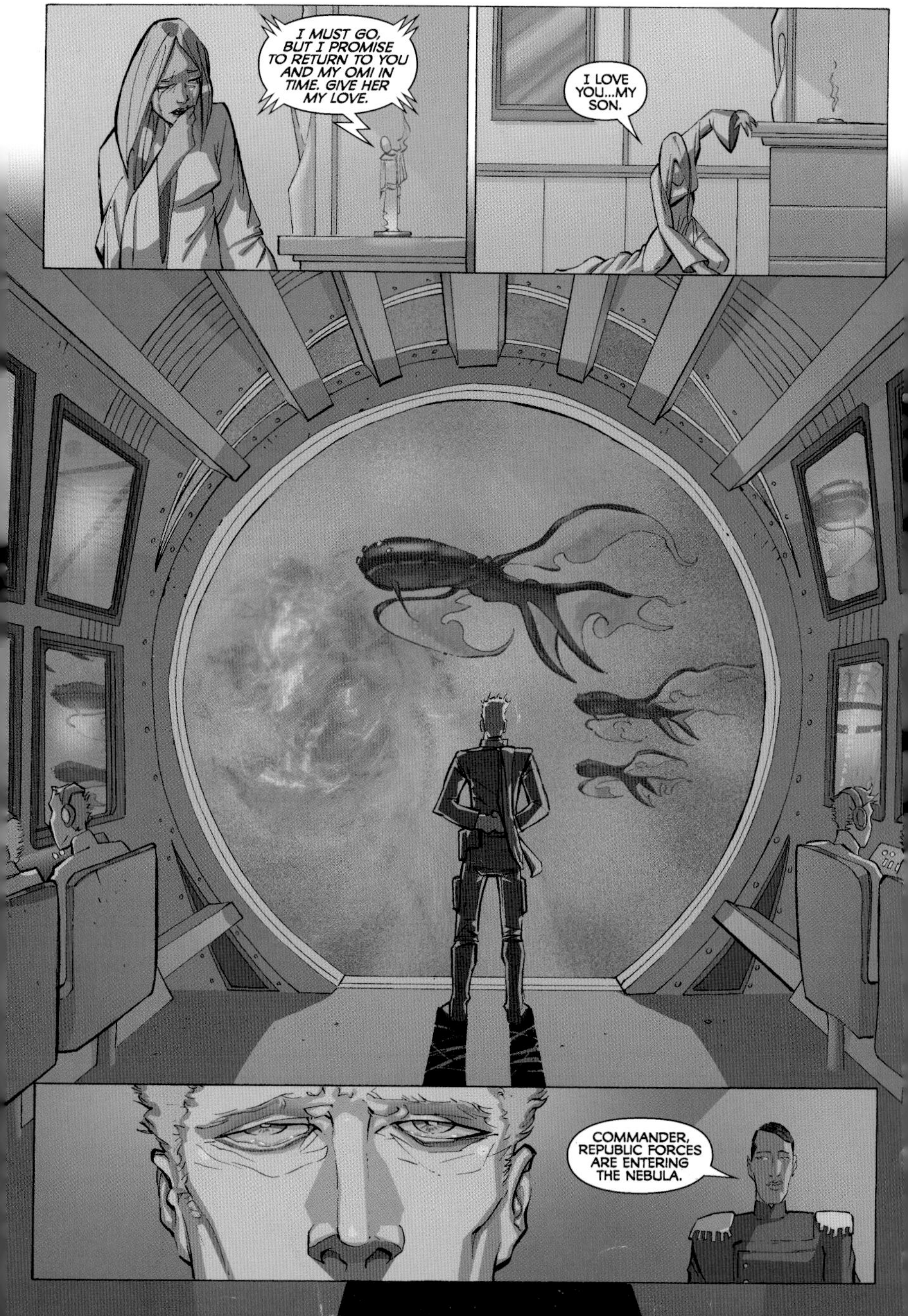
I MUST GO, BUT I PROMISE TO RETURN TO YOU AND MY OMI IN TIME. GIVE HER MY LOVE.
I LOVE YOU...MY SON.
COMMANDER, REPUBLIC FORCES ARE ENTERING THE NEBULA.

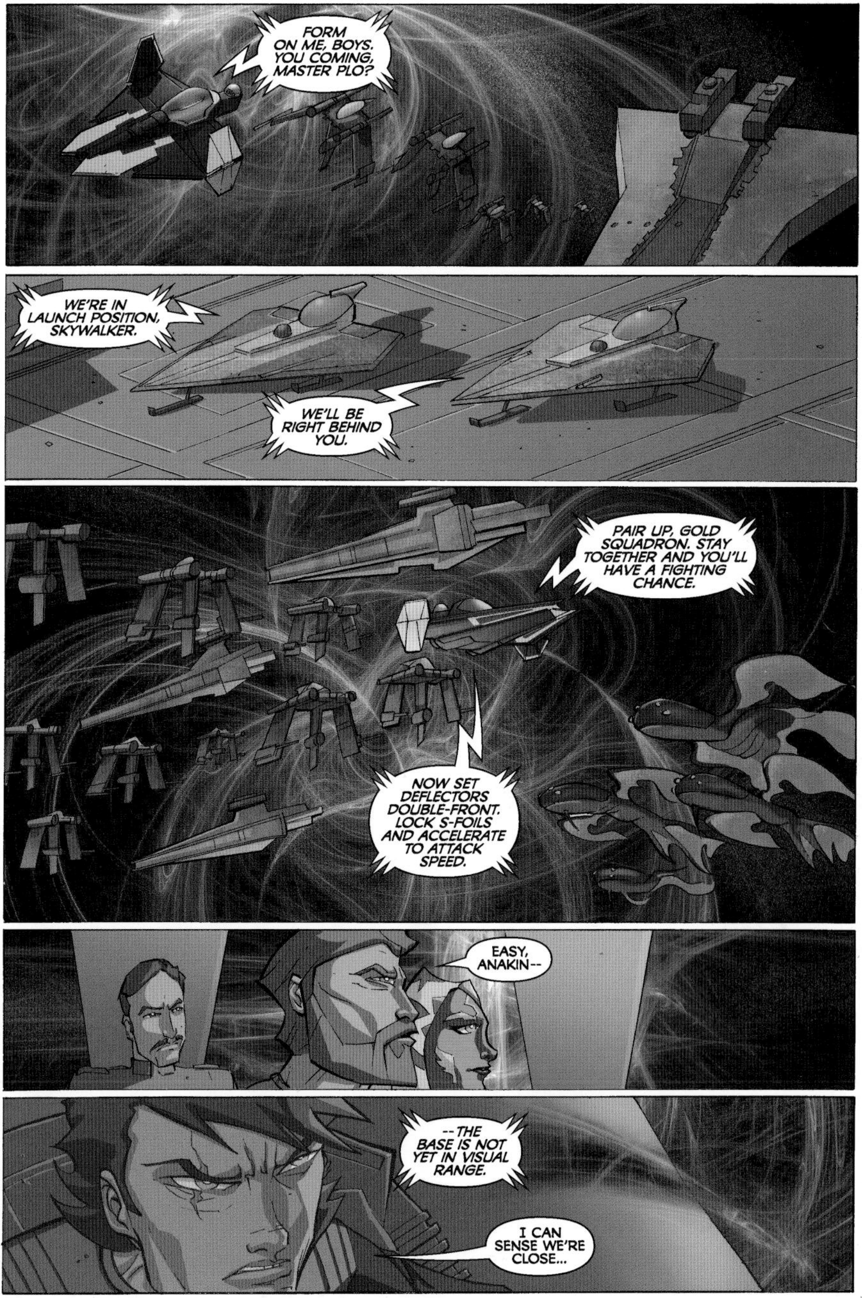
FORM ON ME, BOYS. YOU COMING, MASTER PLO?
WE'RE IN LAUNCH POSITION, SKYWALKER.
WE'LL BE RIGHT BEHIND YOU.
PAIR UP, GOLD SQUADRON. STAY TOGETHER AND YOU'LL HAVE A FIGHTING CHANCE.
NOW SET DEFLECTORS DOUBLE-FRONT. LOCK S-FOILS AND ACCELERATE TO ATTACK SPEED.
EASY, ANAKIN--
--THE BASE IS NOT YET IN VISUAL RANGE.
I CAN SENSE WE'RE CLOSE...

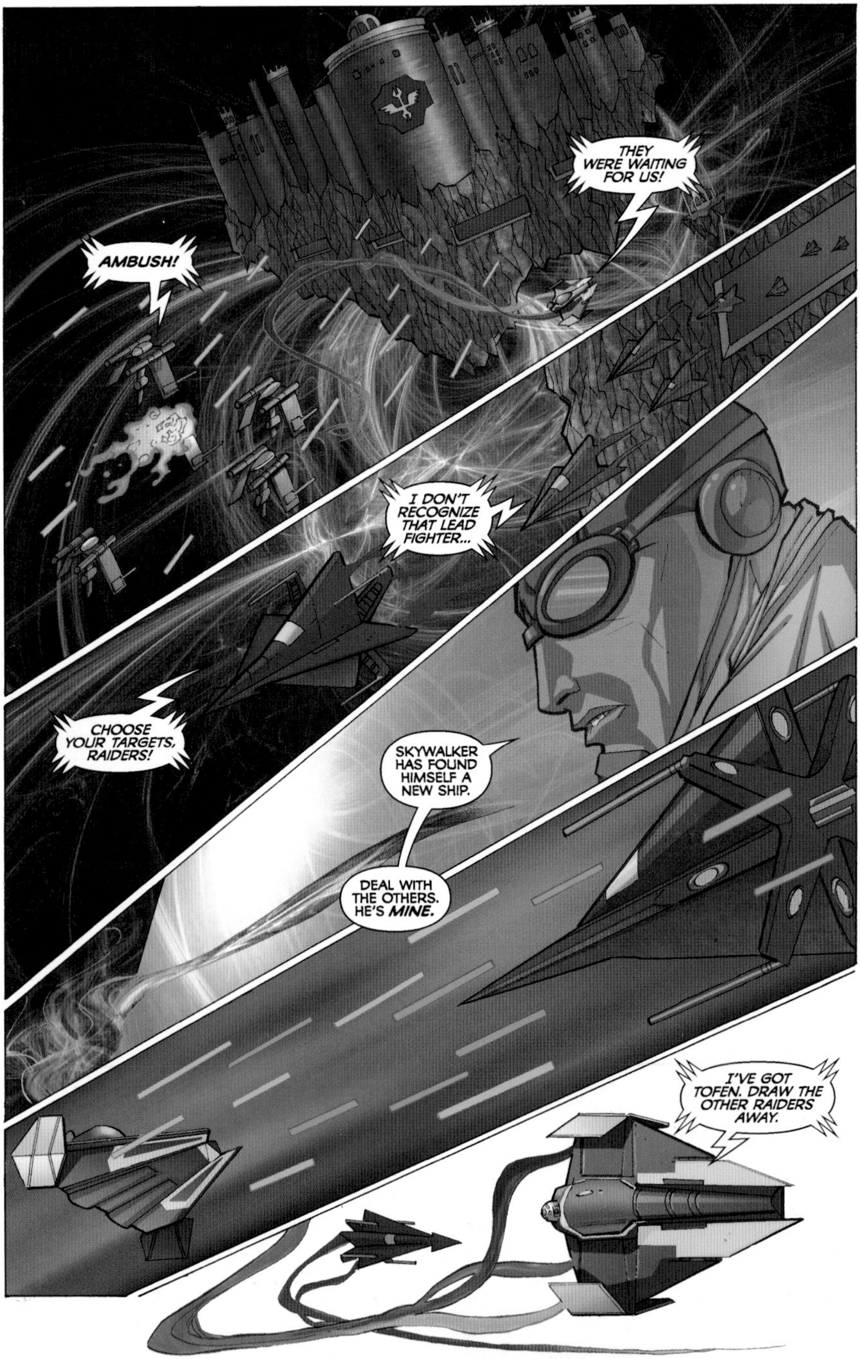
AMBUSH!
THEY WERE WAITING FOR US!
I DON'T RECOGNIZE THAT LEAD FIGHTER...
CHOOSE YOUR TARGETS, RAIDERS!
SKYWALKER HAS FOUND HIMSELF A NEW SHIP.
DEAL WITH THE OTHERS. HE'S MINE.
I'VE GOT TOFEN. DRAW THE OTHER RAIDERS AWAY.

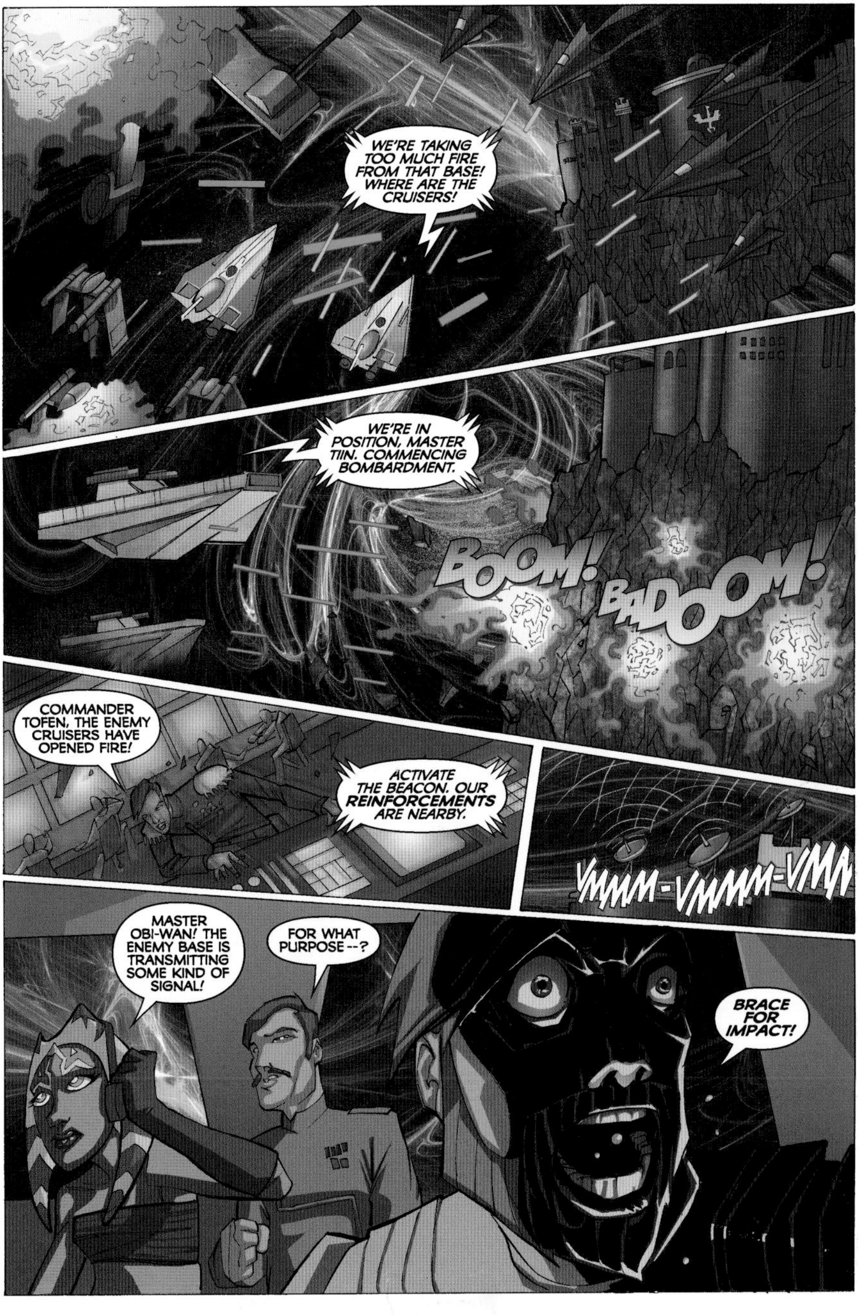
WE'RE TAKING TOO MUCH FIRE FROM THAT BASE! WHERE ARE THE CRUISERS!
WE'RE IN POSITION, MASTER TIIN. COMMENCING BOMBARDMENT.
BOOM! BADOOM!
COMMANDER TOFEN, THE ENEMY CRUISERS HAVE OPENED FIRE!
ACTIVATE THE BEACON. OUR REINFORCEMENTS ARE NEARBY.
VMMM-VMMM-VMM
MASTER OBI-WAN! THE ENEMY BASE IS TRANSMITTING SOME KIND OF SIGNAL!
FOR WHAT PURPOSE--?
BRACE FOR IMPACT!

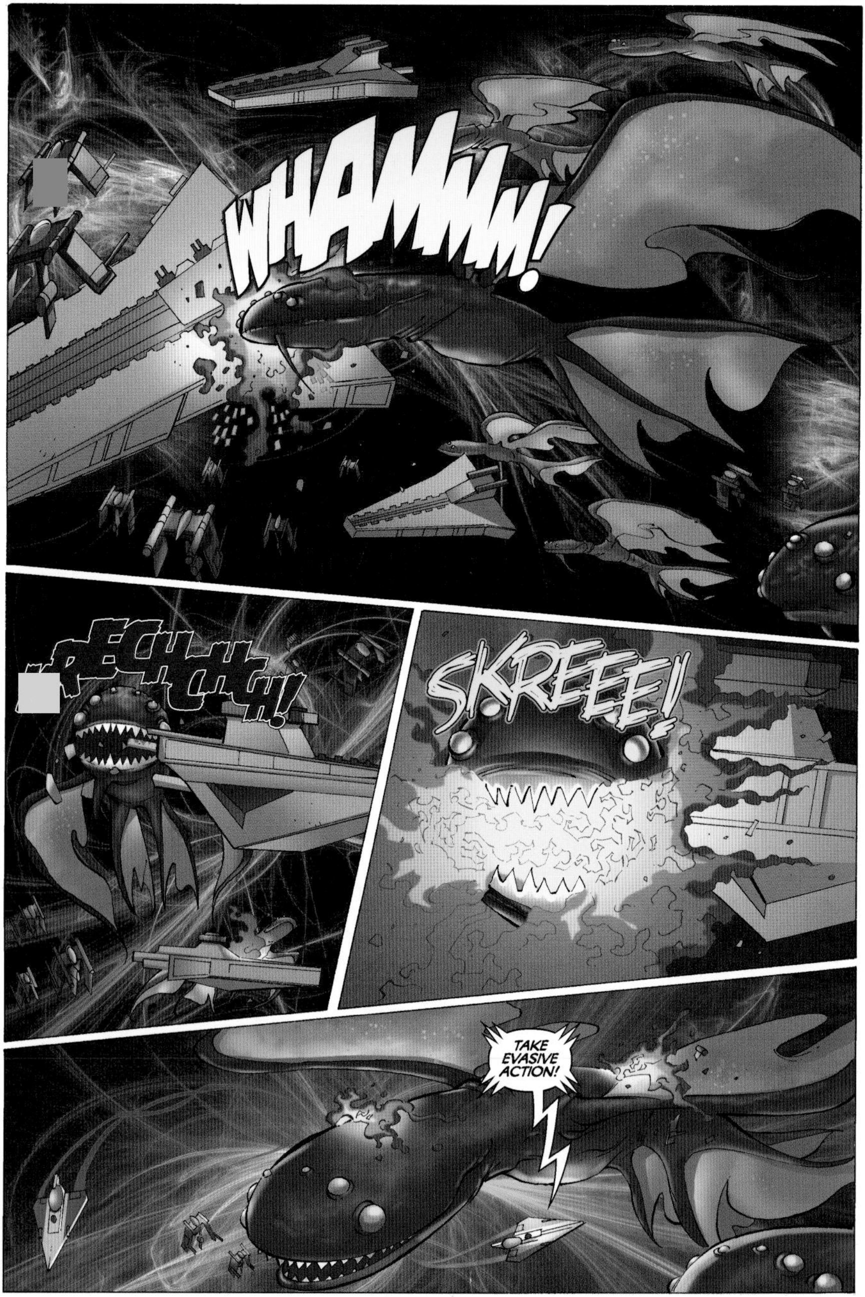
WHAMMM!
SKREEE!
TAKE EVASIVE ACTION!

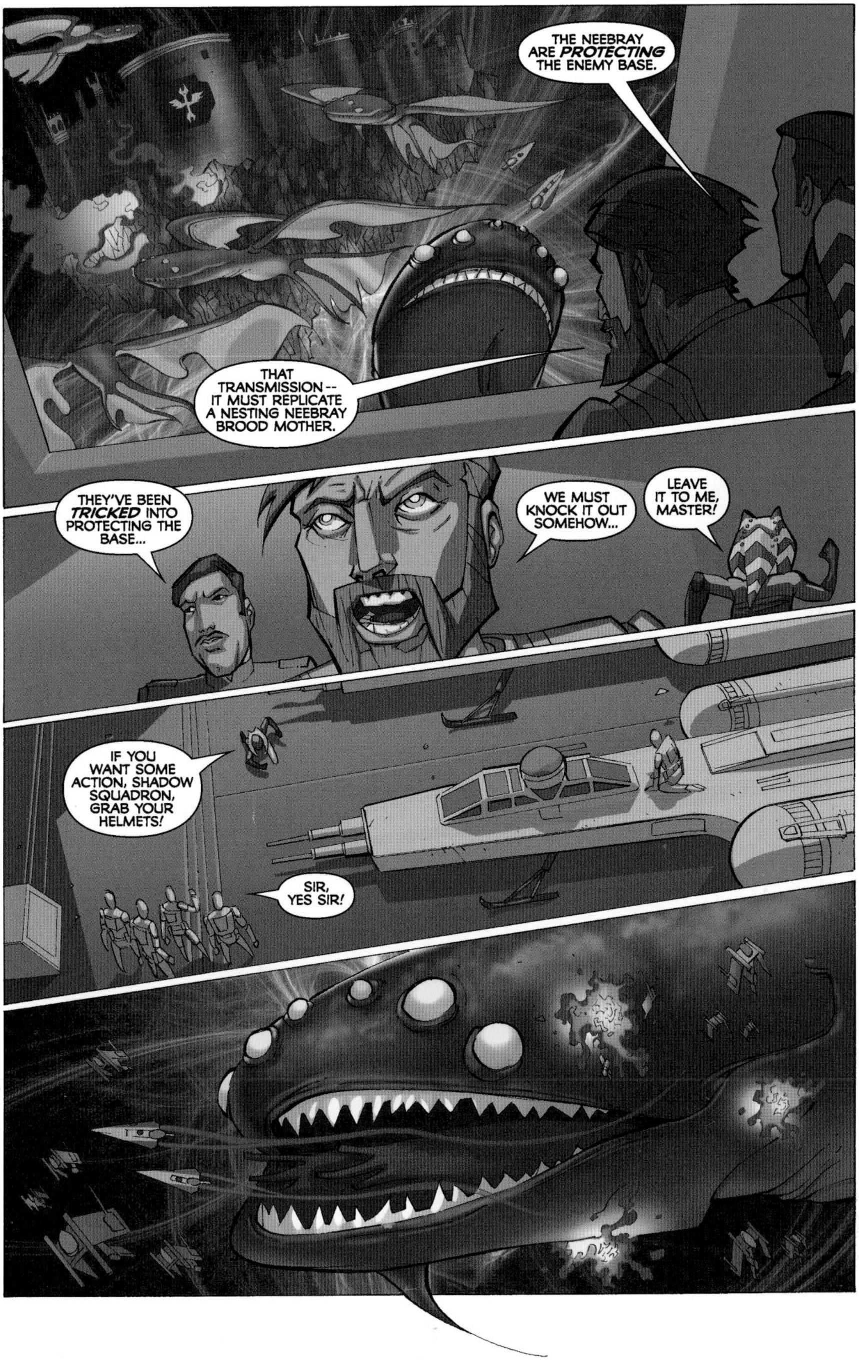
THE NEEBRAY ARE *PROTECTING* THE ENEMY BASE.
THAT TRANSMISSION -- IT MUST REPLICATE A NESTING NEEBRAY BROOD MOTHER.
THEY'VE BEEN *TRICKED* INTO PROTECTING THE BASE...
WE MUST KNOCK IT OUT SOMEHOW...
LEAVE IT TO ME, MASTER!
IF YOU WANT SOME ACTION, SHADOW SQUADRON, GRAB YOUR HELMETS!
SIR, YES SIR!

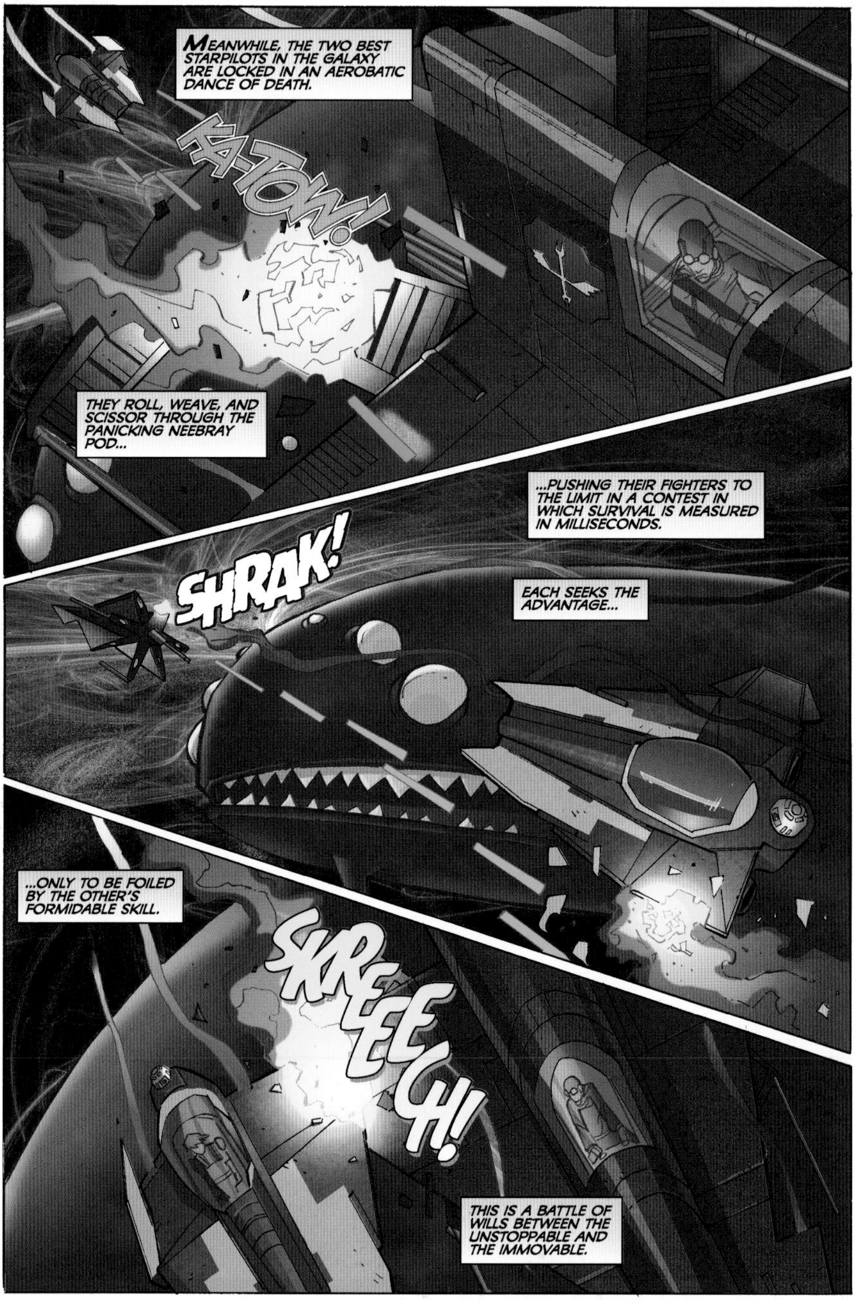
MEANWHILE, THE TWO BEST STARPILOTS IN THE GALAXY ARE LOCKED IN AN AEROBATIC DANCE OF DEATH.
KA-TOW!
THEY ROLL, WEAVE, AND SCISSOR THROUGH THE PANICKING NEEBRAY POD...
...PUSHING THEIR FIGHTERS TO THE LIMIT IN A CONTEST IN WHICH SURVIVAL IS MEASURED IN MILLISECONDS.
SHRAK!
EACH SEEKS THE ADVANTAGE...
...ONLY TO BE FOILED BY THE OTHER'S FORMIDABLE SKILL.
SKREEECH!
THIS IS A BATTLE OF WILLS BETWEEN THE UNSTOPPABLE AND THE IMMOVABLE.

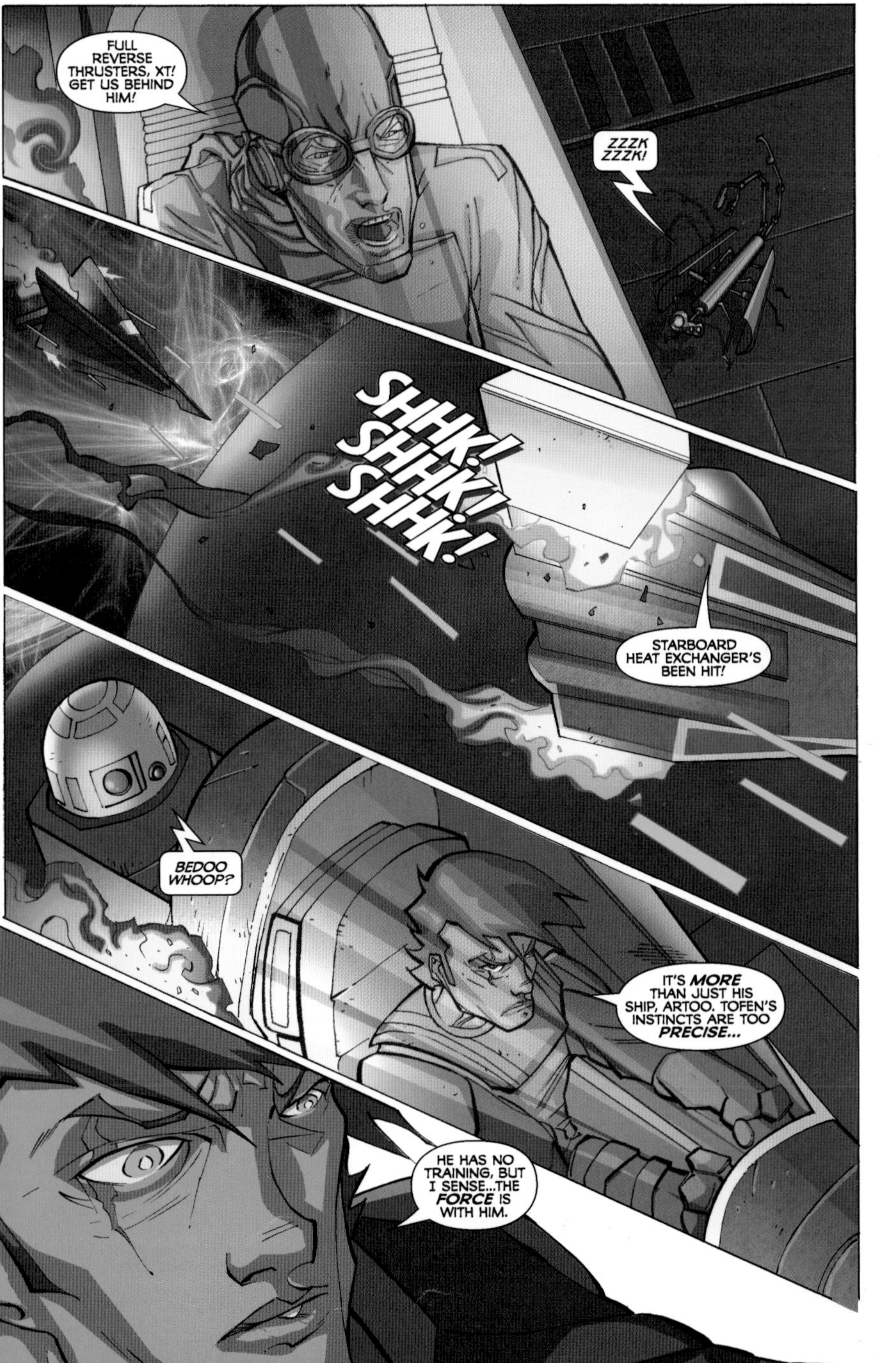

FULL REVERSE THRUSTERS, XT! GET US BEHIND HIM!
ZZZK ZZZK!
SHHK! SHHK! SHHK!
STARBOARD HEAT EXCHANGER'S BEEN HIT!
BEDOO WHOOP?
IT'S *MORE* THAN JUST HIS SHIP, ARTOO. TOFEN'S INSTINCTS ARE TOO *PRECISE...*
HE HAS NO TRAINING, BUT I SENSE...THE *FORCE* IS WITH HIM.

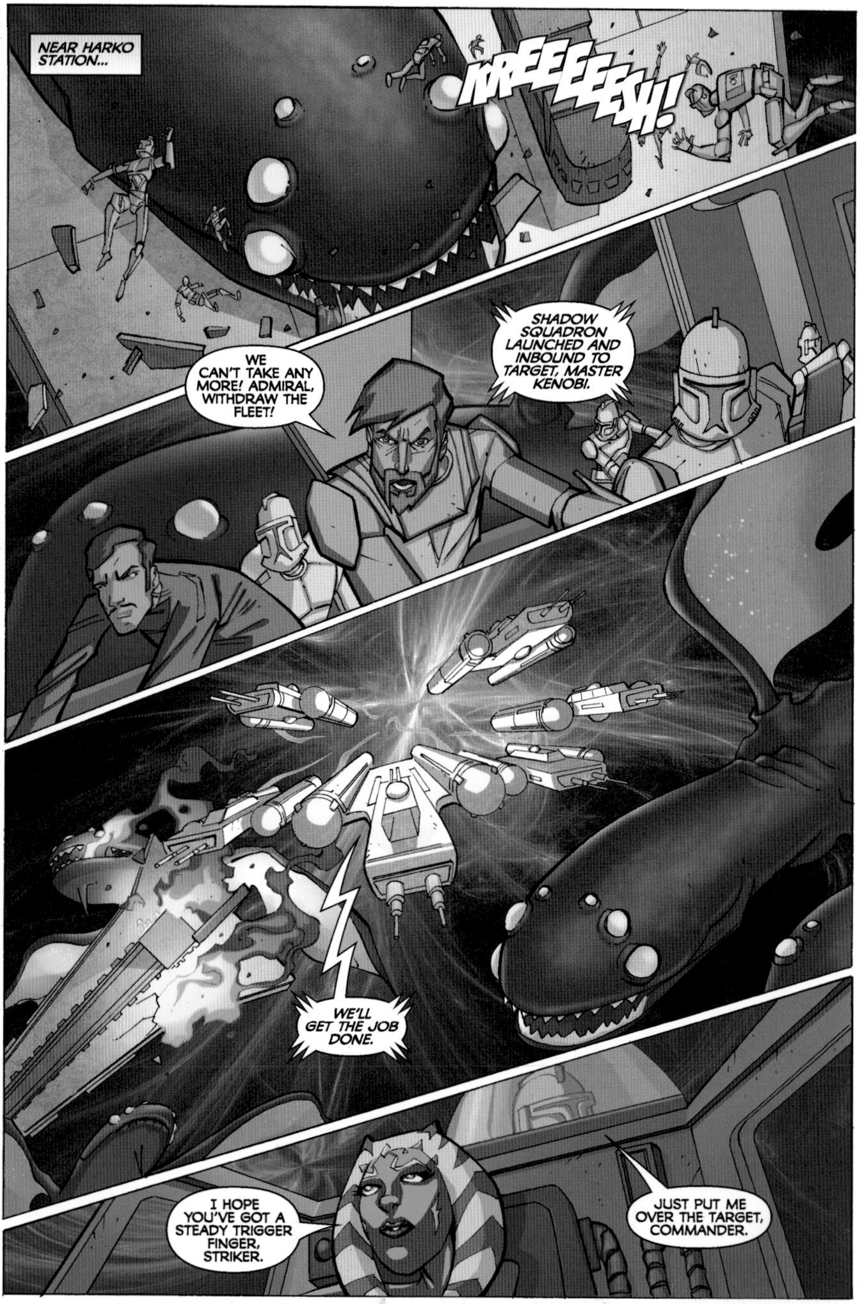
NEAR HARKO STATION...
KREEEEEESH!
WE CAN'T TAKE ANY MORE! ADMIRAL, WITHDRAW THE FLEET!
SHADOW SQUADRON LAUNCHED AND INBOUND TO TARGET, MASTER KENOBI.
WE'LL GET THE JOB DONE.
I HOPE YOU'VE GOT A STEADY TRIGGER FINGER, STRIKER.
JUST PUT ME OVER THE TARGET, COMMANDER.

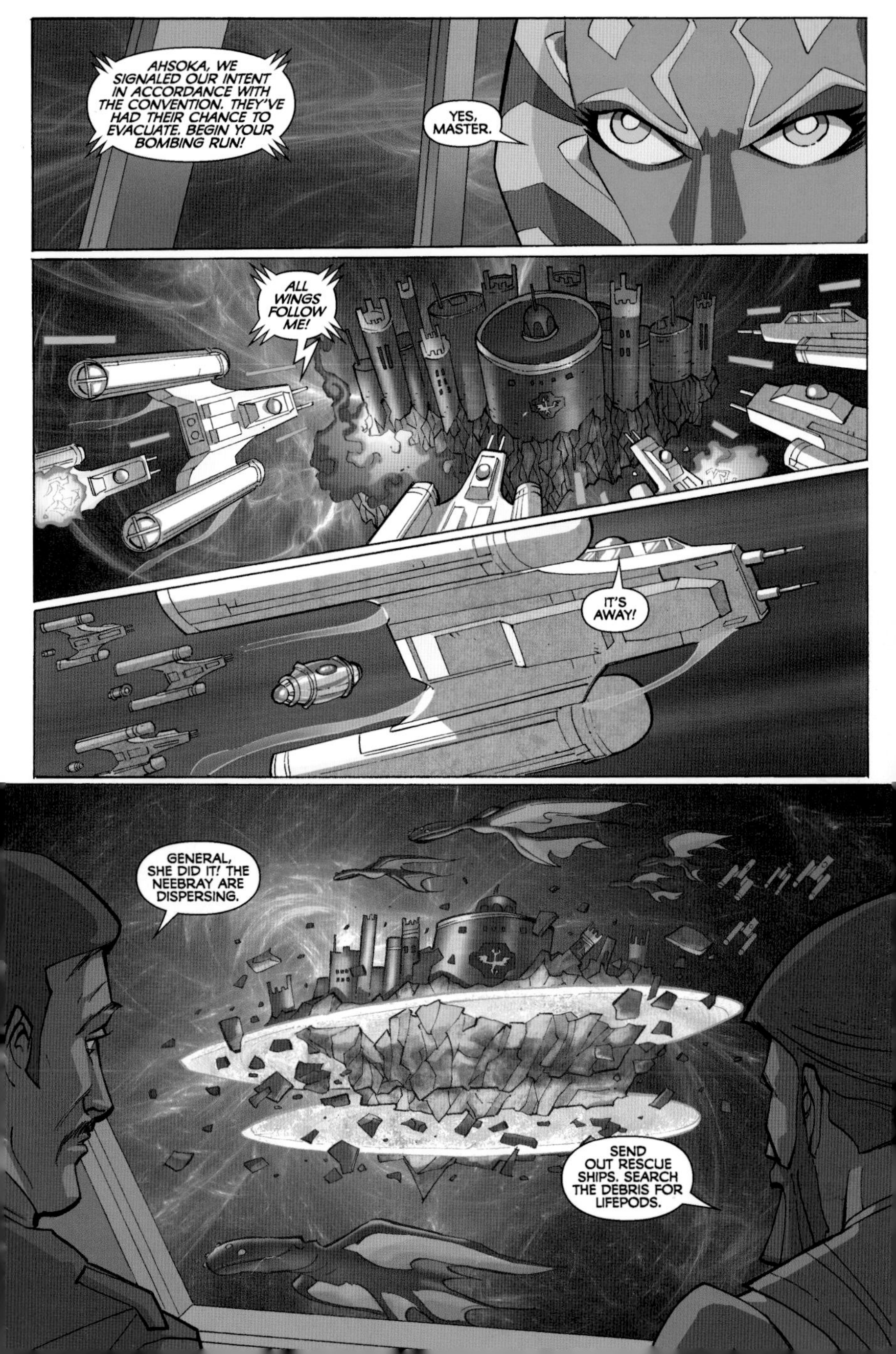
AHSOKA, WE SIGNALED OUR INTENT IN ACCORDANCE WITH THE CONVENTION. THEY'VE HAD THEIR CHANCE TO EVACUATE. BEGIN YOUR BOMBING RUN!
YES, MASTER.
ALL WINGS FOLLOW ME!
IT'S AWAY!
GENERAL, SHE DID IT! THE NEEBRAY ARE DISPERSING.
SEND OUT RESCUE SHIPS. SEARCH THE DEBRIS FOR LIFEPODS.

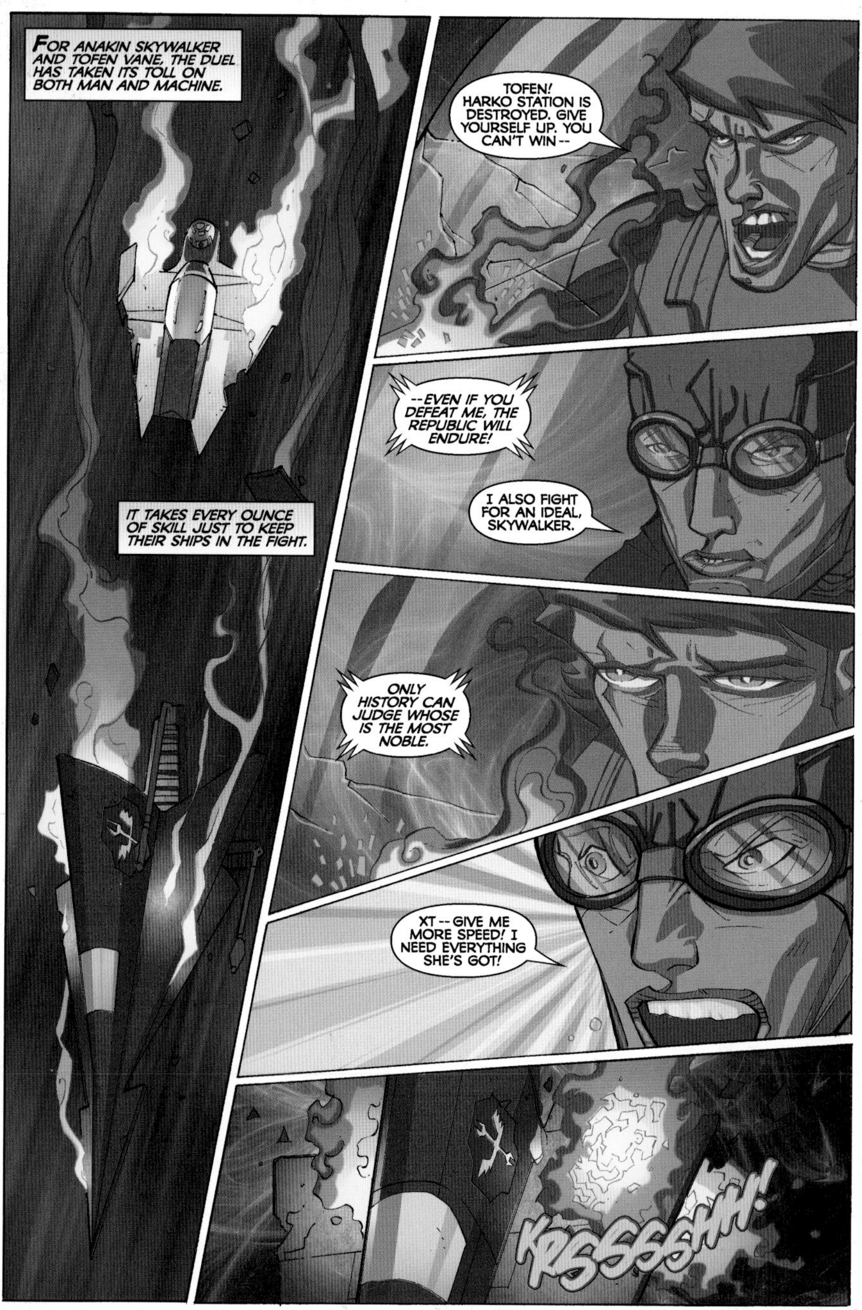
FOR ANAKIN SKYWALKER AND TOFEN VANE, THE DUEL HAS TAKEN ITS TOLL ON BOTH MAN AND MACHINE.
IT TAKES EVERY OUNCE OF SKILL JUST TO KEEP THEIR SHIPS IN THE FIGHT.
TOFEN! HARKO STATION IS DESTROYED. GIVE YOURSELF UP. YOU CAN'T WIN--
--EVEN IF YOU DEFEAT ME, THE REPUBLIC WILL ENDURE!
I ALSO FIGHT FOR AN IDEAL, SKYWALKER.
ONLY HISTORY CAN JUDGE WHOSE IS THE MOST NOBLE.
XT--GIVE ME MORE SPEED! I NEED EVERYTHING SHE'S GOT!
KRSSSSHH!

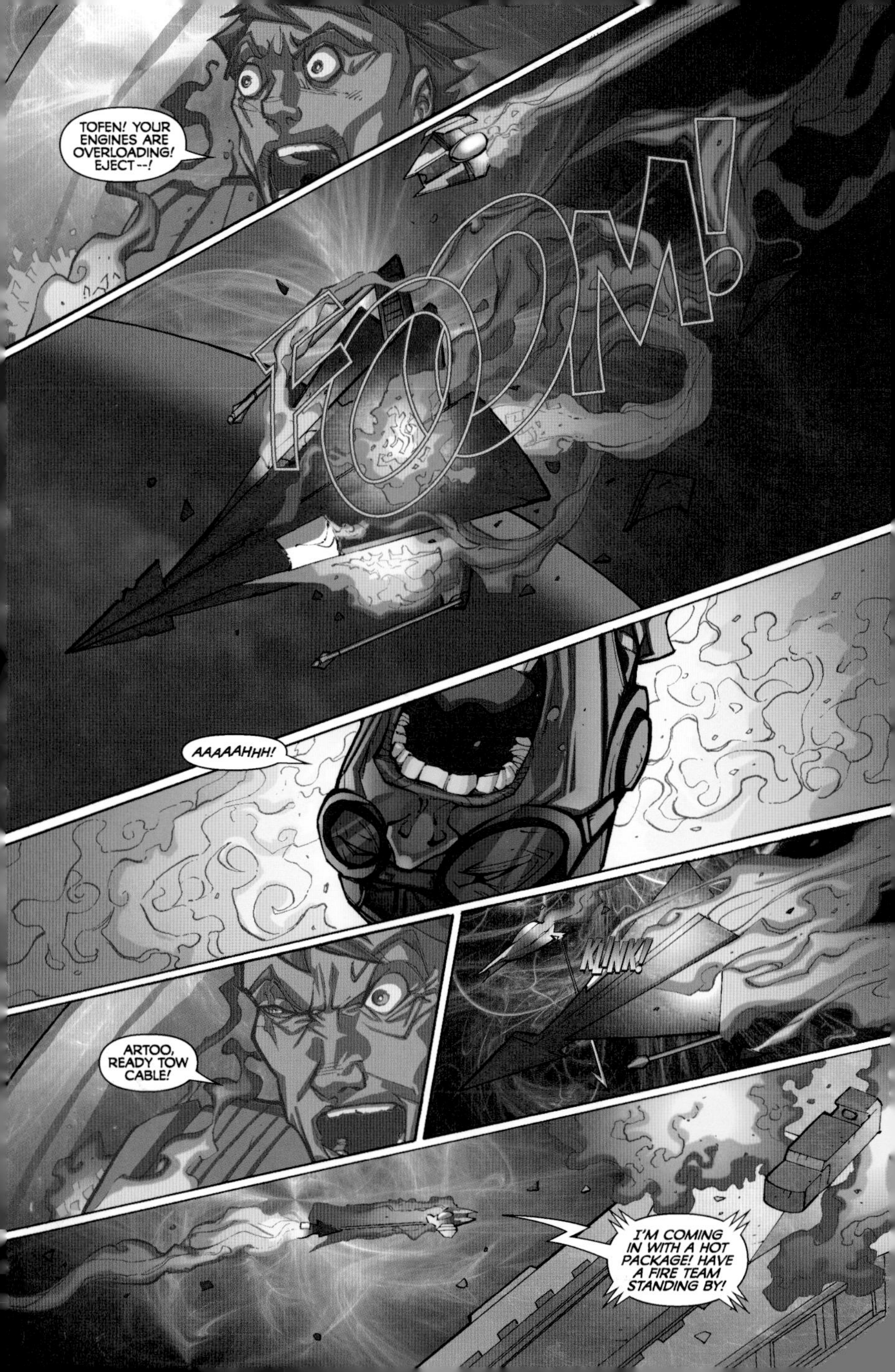
TOFEN! YOUR ENGINES ARE OVERLOADING! EJECT --!
FOOM!
AAAAAHHH!
KLINK!
ARTOO, READY TOW CABLE!
I'M COMING IN WITH A HOT PACKAGE! HAVE A FIRE TEAM STANDING BY!

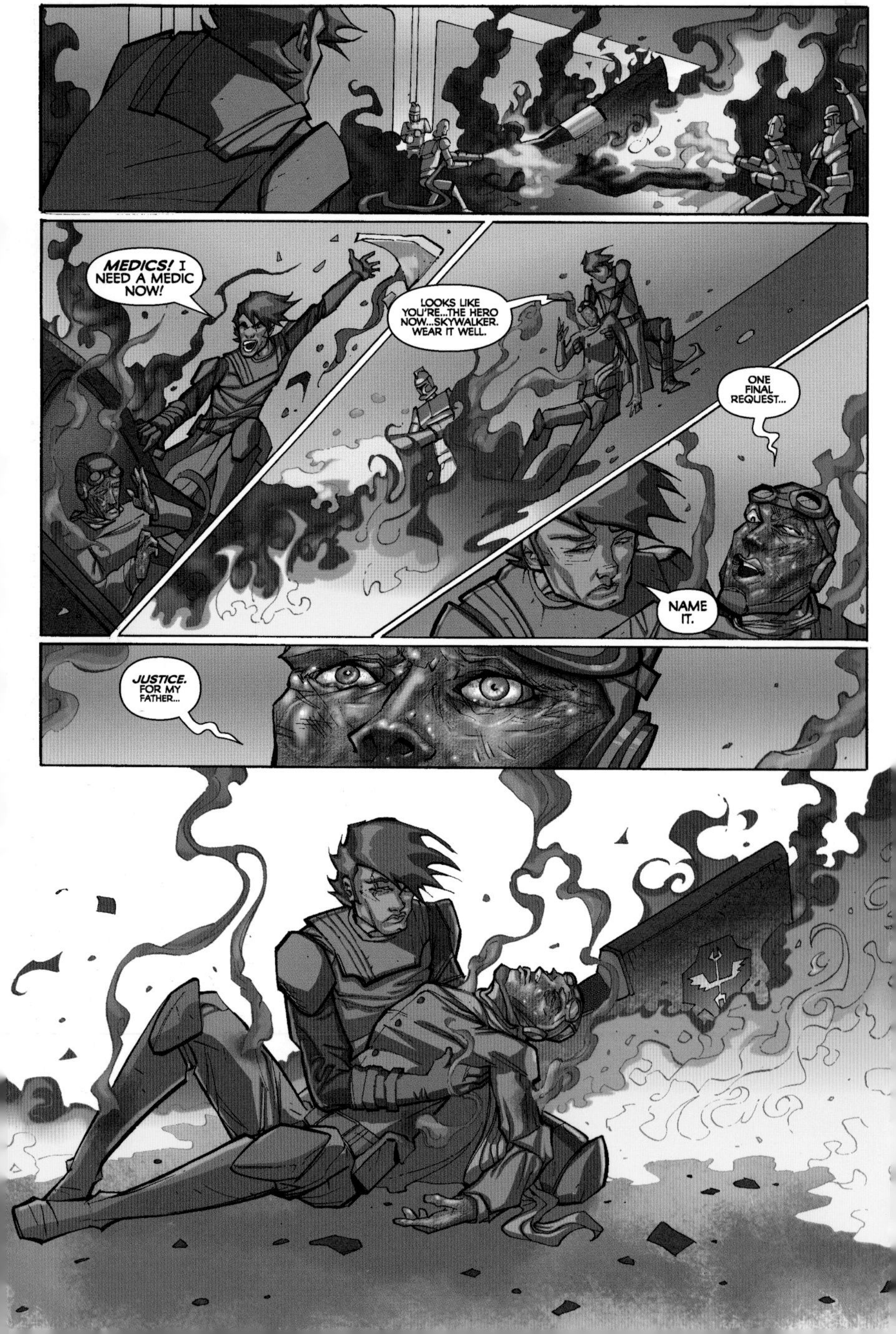
MEDICS! I NEED A MEDIC NOW!
LOOKS LIKE YOU'RE...THE HERO NOW...SKYWALKER. WEAR IT WELL.
ONE FINAL REQUEST...
NAME IT.
JUSTICE. FOR MY FATHER...

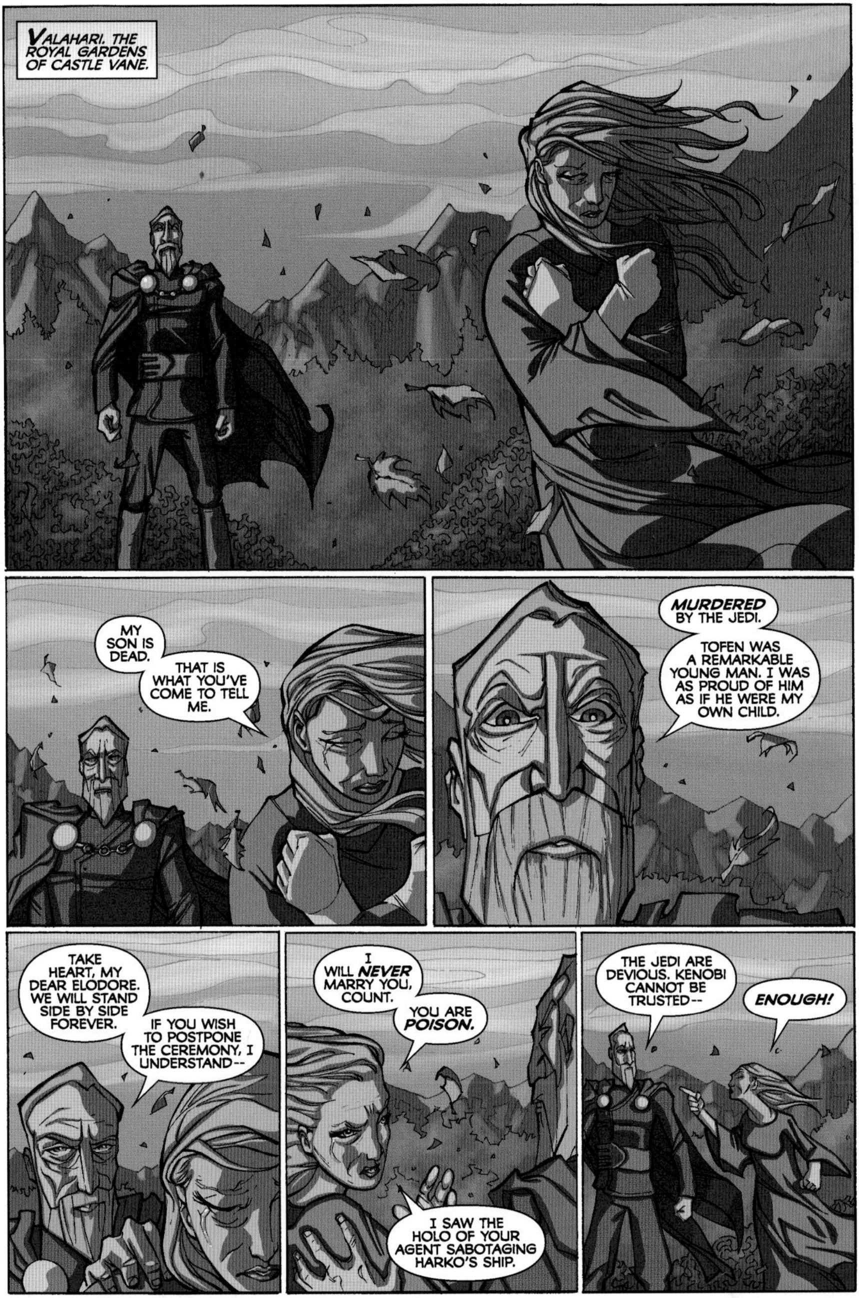
VALAHARI. THE ROYAL GARDENS OF CASTLE VANE.
MY SON IS DEAD.
THAT IS WHAT YOU'VE COME TO TELL ME.
MURDERED BY THE JEDI.
TOFEN WAS A REMARKABLE YOUNG MAN. I WAS AS PROUD OF HIM AS IF HE WERE MY OWN CHILD.
TAKE HEART, MY DEAR ELODORE. WE WILL STAND SIDE BY SIDE FOREVER.
IF YOU WISH TO POSTPONE THE CEREMONY, I UNDERSTAND--
I WILL NEVER MARRY YOU, COUNT.
YOU ARE POISON.
I SAW THE HOLO OF YOUR AGENT SABOTAGING HARKO'S SHIP.
THE JEDI ARE DEVIOUS. KENOBI CANNOT BE TRUSTED--
ENOUGH!

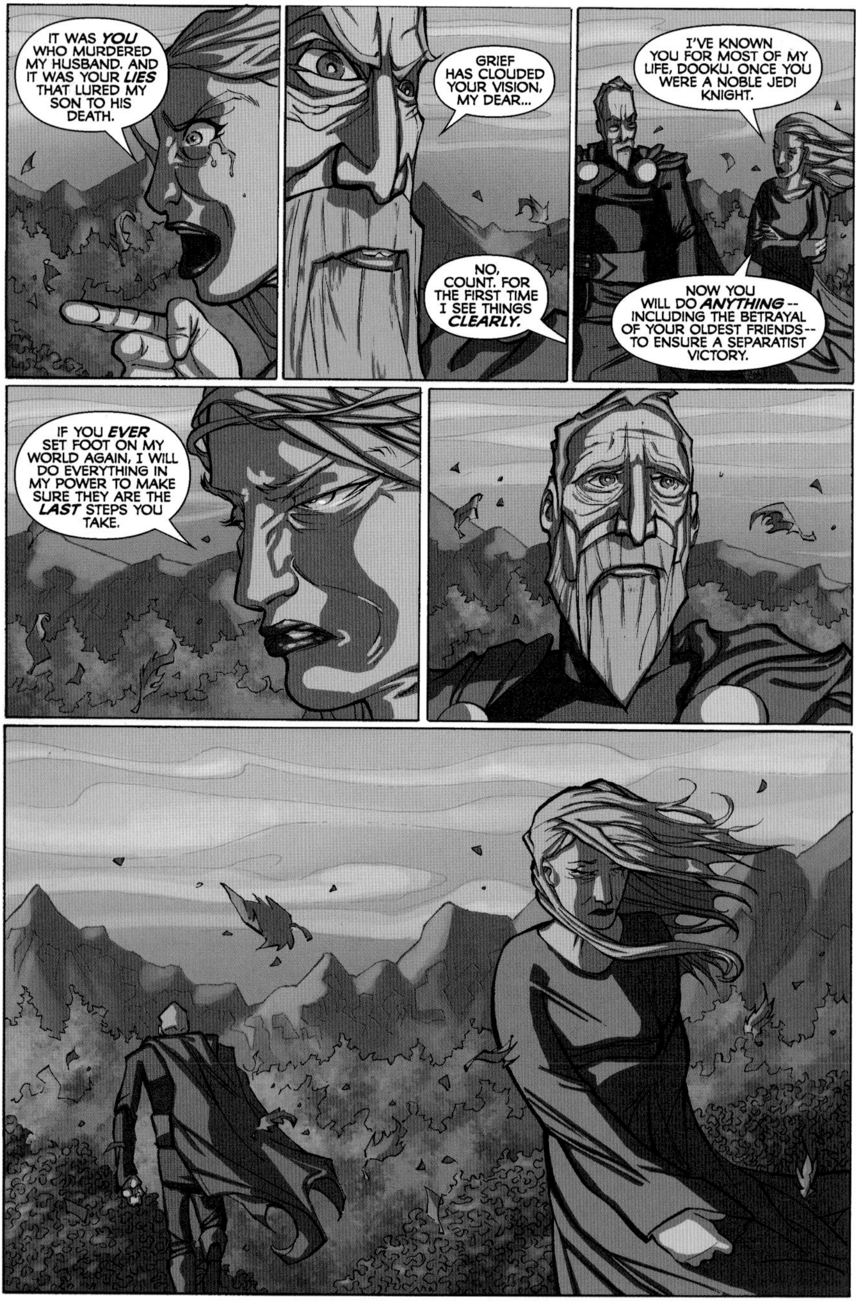
IT WAS *YOU* WHO MURDERED MY HUSBAND. AND IT WAS YOUR *LIES* THAT LURED MY SON TO HIS DEATH.
GRIEF HAS CLOUDED YOUR VISION, MY DEAR...
NO, COUNT. FOR THE FIRST TIME I SEE THINGS *CLEARLY.*
I'VE KNOWN YOU FOR MOST OF MY LIFE, DOOKU. ONCE YOU WERE A NOBLE JEDI KNIGHT.
NOW YOU WILL DO *ANYTHING* -- INCLUDING THE BETRAYAL OF YOUR OLDEST FRIENDS-- TO ENSURE A SEPARATIST VICTORY.
IF YOU *EVER* SET FOOT ON MY WORLD AGAIN, I WILL DO EVERYTHING IN MY POWER TO MAKE SURE THEY ARE THE *LAST* STEPS YOU TAKE.

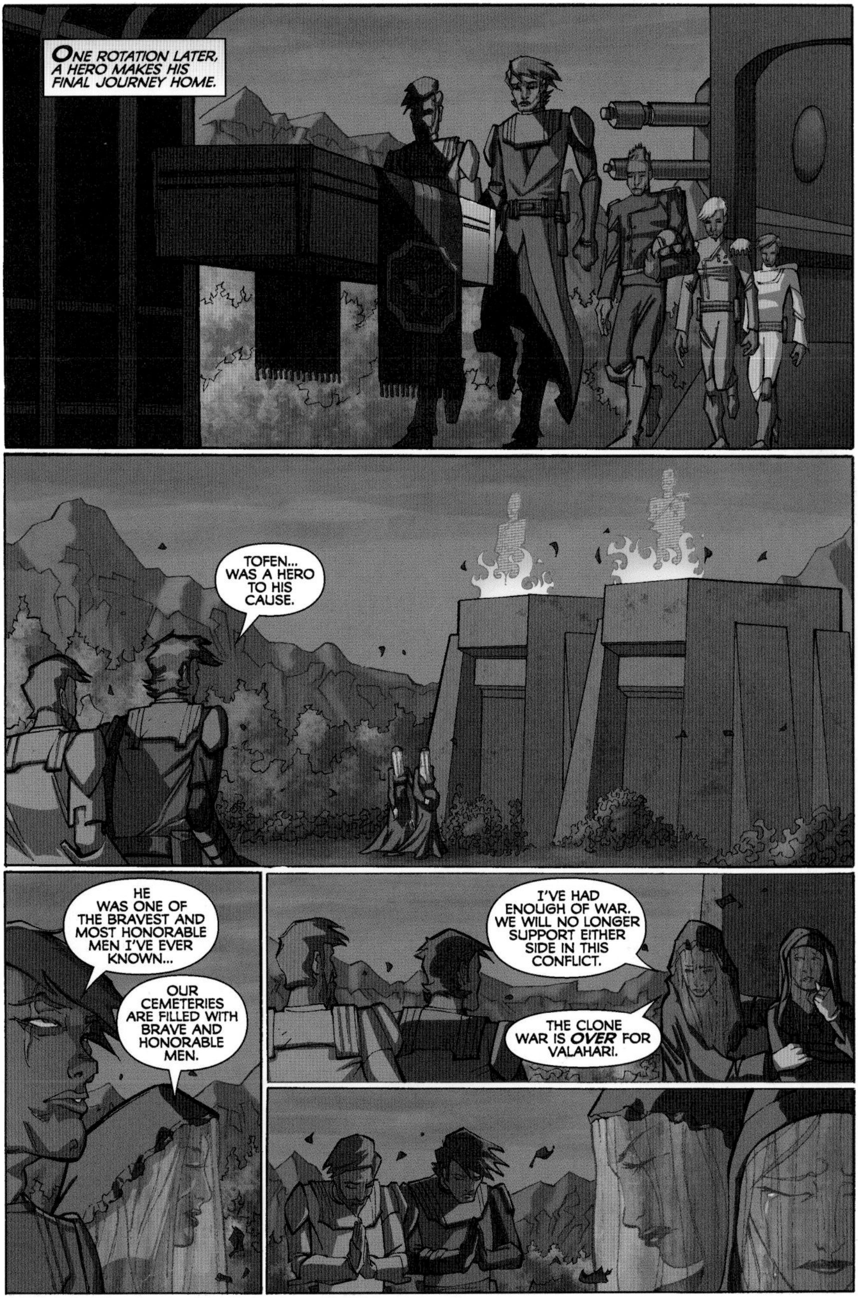
ONE ROTATION LATER, A HERO MAKES HIS FINAL JOURNEY HOME.
TOFEN... WAS A HERO TO HIS CAUSE.
HE WAS ONE OF THE BRAVEST AND MOST HONORABLE MEN I'VE EVER KNOWN...
OUR CEMETERIES ARE FILLED WITH BRAVE AND HONORABLE MEN.
I'VE HAD ENOUGH OF WAR. WE WILL NO LONGER SUPPORT EITHER SIDE IN THIS CONFLICT.
THE CLONE WAR IS *OVER* FOR VALAHARI.

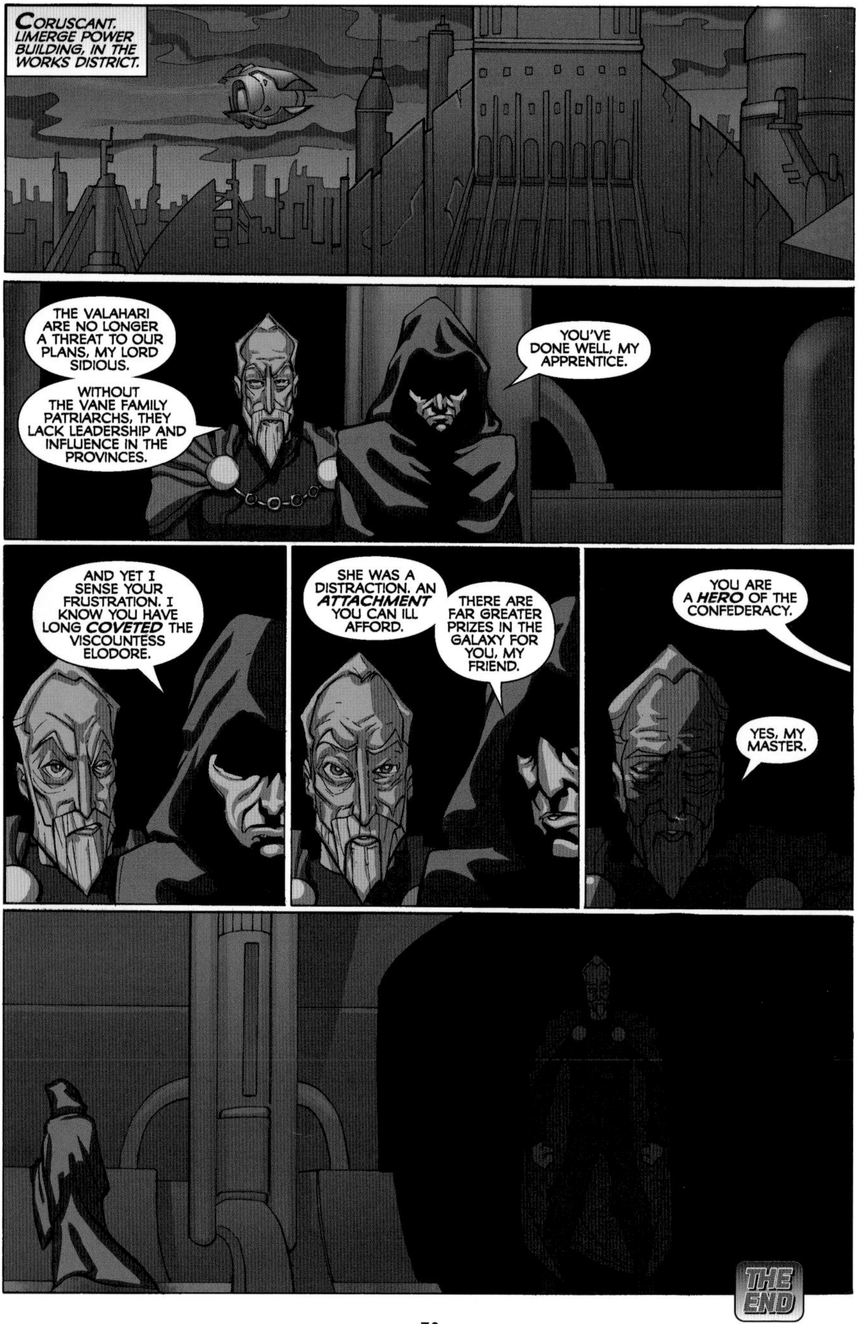
CORUSCANT. LIMERGE POWER BUILDING, IN THE WORKS DISTRICT.
THE VALAHARI ARE NO LONGER A THREAT TO OUR PLANS, MY LORD SIDIOUS.
WITHOUT THE VANE FAMILY PATRIARCHS, THEY LACK LEADERSHIP AND INFLUENCE IN THE PROVINCES.
YOU'VE DONE WELL, MY APPRENTICE.
AND YET I SENSE YOUR FRUSTRATION. I KNOW YOU HAVE LONG COVETED THE VISCOUNTESS ELODORE.
SHE WAS A DISTRACTION. AN ATTACHMENT YOU CAN ILL AFFORD.
THERE ARE FAR GREATER PRIZES IN THE GALAXY FOR YOU, MY FRIEND.
YOU ARE A HERO OF THE CONFEDERACY.
YES, MY MASTER.
THE END

STAR WARS GRAPHIC NOVEL TIMELINE (IN YEARS)

Omnibus: Tales of the Jedi—5,000–3,986 BSW4

Knights of the Old Republic (9 volumes)—3,964 BSW4

Jedi vs. Sith—1,000 BSW4

Omnibus: Rise of the Sith—33 BSW4

Episode I: The Phantom Menace—32 BSW4

Omnibus: Emissaries and Assassins—32 BSW4

Bounty Hunters—31 BSW4

Omnibus: Quinlan Vos – Jedi in Darkness—31–28 BSW4

Omnibus: Menace Revealed—31–22 BSW4

Honor and Duty—24 BSW4

Episode II: Attack of the Clones—22 BSW4

Clone Wars (9 volumes)—22–19 BSW4

Clone Wars Adventures (10 volumes)—22–19 BSW4

The Clone Wars (7 volumes)—22–19 BSW4

General Grievous—20 BSW4

Episode III: Revenge of the Sith—19 BSW4

Dark Times (4 volumes)—19 BSW4

Omnibus: Droids—3 BSW4

Omnibus: Boba Fett—3–1 BSW4, 0–10 ASW4

The Force Unleashed—2 BSW4

Adventures (4 volumes)—1–0 BSW4, 0–3 ASW4

Episode IV: A New Hope—SW4

Classic Star Wars—0–3 ASW4

A Long Time Ago… (7 volumes)—0–4 ASW4

Empire (6 volumes)—0 ASW4

Rebellion (3 volumes)—0 ASW4

Omnibus: Early Victories—0–1 ASW4

Jabba the Hutt: The Art of the Deal—1 ASW4

Episode V: The Empire Strikes Back—3 ASW4

Omnibus: Shadows of the Empire—3.5–4.5 ASW4

Episode VI: Return of the Jedi—4 ASW4

Omnibus: X-Wing Rogue Squadron—4–5 ASW4

The Thrawn Trilogy—9 ASW4

Dark Empire—10 ASW4

Crimson Empire—11 ASW4

Jedi Academy: Leviathan—13 ASW4

Union—20 ASW4

Chewbacca—25 ASW4

Legacy (10 volumes)—130 ASW4

Old Republic Era
25,000 – 1000 years before
Star Wars: A New Hope

Rise of the Empire Era
1000 – 0 years before
Star Wars: A New Hope

Rebellion Era
0 – 5 years after
Star Wars: A New Hope

New Republic Era
5 – 25 years after
Star Wars: A New Hope

New Jedi Order Era
25+ years after
Star Wars: A New Hope

Legacy Era
130+ years after
Star Wars: A New Hope

Infinities
Does not apply to timeline

Sergio Aragonés Stomps Star Wars
Star Wars Tales
Star Wars Infinities
Tag and Bink
Star Wars Visionaries

BSW4 = before *Episode IV: A New Hope*. ASW4 = after *Episode IV: A New Hope*.

FOR MORE ADVENTURE IN A GALAXY FAR, FAR, AWAY . . .

STAR WARS
ADVENTURES
HAN SOLO AND THE
HOLLOW MOON OF KHORYA

STAR WARS
ADVENTURES
PRINCESS LEIA AND
THE ROYAL RANSOM

STAR WARS
ADVENTURES
LUKE SKYWALKER AND THE
TREASURE OF THE DRAGONSNAKES

STAR WARS
THE CLONE WARS
THE COLOSSUS OF DESTINY

STAR WARS ADVENTURES: HAN SOLO AND THE HOLLOW MOON OF KHORYA
978-1-59582-198-0 | $7.99

STAR WARS ADVENTURES: PRINCESS LEIA AND THE ROYAL RANSOM
978-1-59582-147-8 | $7.99

STAR WARS ADVENTURES: LUKE SKYWALKER AND THE TREASURE OF THE DRAGONSNAKES
978-1-59582-347-2 | $7.99

STAR WARS: THE CLONE WARS— THE COLOSSUS OF DESTINY
978-1-59582-416-5 | $7.9

STAR WARS
THE CLONE WARS
SHIPYARDS OF DOOM

STAR WARS
THE CLONE WARS
CRASH COURSE

STAR WARS
THE CLONE WARS
THE WIND RAIDERS OF TALORAAN

STAR WARS
THE CLONE WARS
SLAVES OF THE REPUBLIC

STAR WARS: THE CLONE WARS— SHIPYARDS OF DOOM
978-1-59582-207-9 | $7.99

STAR WARS: THE CLONE WARS—CRASH COURSE
978-1-59582-230-7 | $7.99

STAR WARS: THE CLONE WARS— THE WIND RAIDERS OF TALORAAN
978-1-59582-231-4 | $7.99

STAR WARS: THE CLONE WARS— SLAVES OF THE REPUBLIC
978-1-59582-349-6 | $9.9

DARK HORSE BOOKS
darkhorse.com

AVAILABLE AT YOUR LOCAL COMICS SHOP OR BOOKSTORE

To find a comics shop in your area, call 1-888-266-4226
For more information or to order direct: • On the web: darkhorse.com • E-mail: mailorder@darkhor
• Phone: 1-800-862-0052 Mon.–Fri. 9 AM to 5 PM Pacific Time.

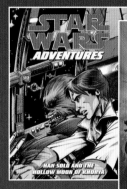

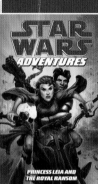

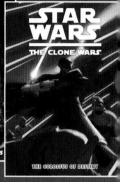

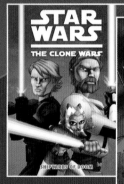

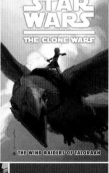

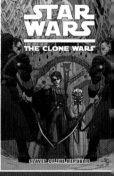

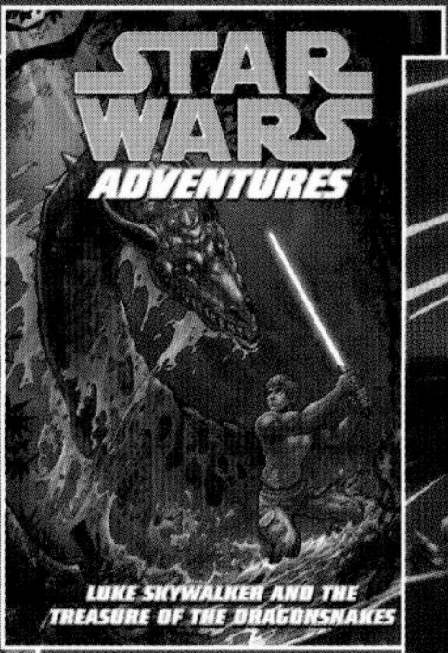

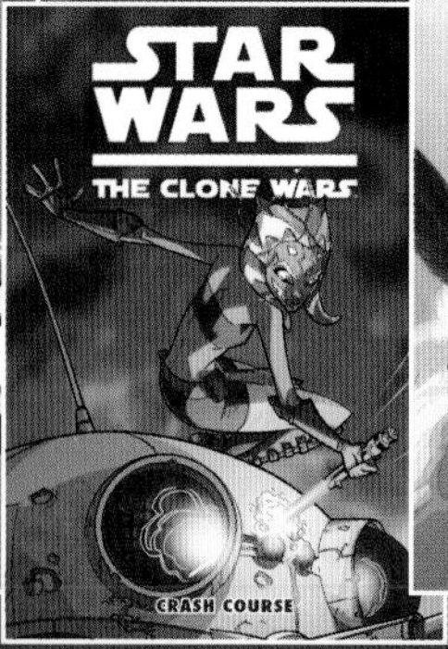